WHAT HAPPENED TO ICARUS

WHAT HAPPENED TO ICARUS

*Encountering the Unfathomable
in a World in Crisis*

THEODORE RICHARDS

WAYFARER BOOKS
SAN JUAN MOUNTAINS, COLORADO

WAYFARER BOOKS
SAN JUAN MOUNTAINS, COLORADO

© 2026 text by Theodore Richards

Some names and identifying details have been changed to protect the privacy of individuals.

Wayfarer Books supports copyright. Copyright fuels creativity, encourages diverse voices, promotes free speech, and creates a vibrant culture. Thank you for buying an authorized edition of this book and for complying with copyright laws by not reproducing, scanning, or distributing any part of it in any form without permission. You are supporting writers and allowing us to continue to publish books for every reader.

All Rights Reserved
First Edition Published in 2026 by Wayfarer Books
Cover Design and Interior Design by Connor Wolfe
Cover Image © Bernard Picart Fall of Icarus, 1731
TRADE PAPERBACK 978-1-965320-93-8
EBOOK 978-1-965320-94-5

10 9 8 7 6 5 4 3 2 1

WHOLESALE INQUIRIES? You can find our books available via Ingram, offered with standard trade terms and lifetime returnability. With printing bases in the US, the EU, the UK, and Australia, Wayfarer has the capability to fulfill orders globally. Our titles are available wherever books are sold in paperback, ebook, and audiobook. Find our books at local Indies, Bookshop.org, iTunes, Barnes & Noble, Amazon > US & International, or direct at wayfarerbookstore.com.

WAYFARERBOOKS.ORG
WAYFARERMAGAZINE.COM
WAYFARERBOOKSTORE.COM

ALSO BY THE AUTHOR

Handprints on the Womb

Cosmosophia

The Crucifixion

The Conversions

Creatively Maladjusted

A Letter to My Daughters

The Great Re-imagining

Re-imagining the Classroom

Dedication

*To my daughters, who've made me pay attention.
And for all those who have fallen
and continue to swim in the depths.*

I want to know what happened to Icarus

after his wings melted away,

when he fell into the fathomless sea.

This is where the story begins.

Tu proverai sì come sa di sale
lo pane altrui, e come è duro calle
lo scendere e 'l salir per l'altrui scale.

You shall find out how salt
is the taste of another man's bread, and how hard
is the way up and down another man's stairs.

—Dante's Paradiso, Canto XVII, lines 58-60.

PROLOGUE
COSMIC SURPRISE
2015

Tell me a story, I will say.

You know all my stories; you've heard them all.

What does that matter? What do you think I'm here for?

What *are* you here for? She'll tease me. I still don't know.

I'm here to hear your stories, the same old stories, over and over again.

"You're gonna have to catch the baby!"

My wife's voice was loud and strained, with a hint of panic. I continued to fumble with the showerhead. Moments before, when she'd realized she was in labor, she'd asked me to attach the hose to the showerhead in order to fill the birthing tub while we waited for the midwife. Our third daughter, Vismaya, whom we'd never expected, was a planned homebirth; but the plan was to have a midwife present.

I fumbled some more. There are things I am good at, things that don't particularly faze me. Plumbing and anything that has to do with taking things apart and putting them back together are not on that list. I let out a sigh of relief. I much preferred to catch a baby than reconfigure the plumbing.

Ari's voice was letting out sounds that had grown increasingly, desperately, primal as Cosima, now seven, came into the bathroom. We'd welcomed her participation in the birth, but she looked a little scared. It was the sounds her mother was making. "You don't have to stay," I said. She went back to her room, got under the covers, and waited for her sister to arrive.

I washed my hands. It seemed like the thing to do. Seemed *medical*.

"I don't think I can do this!" my wife exclaimed, voice cracking just a bit. She must have been thinking some unarticulated version of this: *The midwife isn't here and I am left in the hands of a man who can't unscrew a showerhead, who can't even turn on the television without me. This is why women used to die in childbirth in the 1800s.* And I *did* always joke that, without my wife, our home is like the 1800s, so limited are my technical capabilities.

But there was nothing technical, or even medical, about this birth. I looked her in the eye. "You *can* do this," I said. "You've done this before." Like this was what we'd been waiting to do since that day, so many years ago, on the porch: to give birth. *Like this was the rhyme she'd been waiting to spit but couldn't quite find the words until now.*

She focused on pushing. I felt beneath where she squatted. Drops of blood fell over my hands, then more. Then the head. The head is the hardest part, the most painful part, as anyone knows who has given birth or witnessed a birth. It is the uniquely human part of the process; our big heads contain the minds that contain universes, from the cave paintings to Coltrane. We think we are different merely because our big heads make us smarter. But the human baby is born earlier, less developed, than it should be. Any longer a gestation period and the head would never get through. So we don't get up running like zebras.

Those who have witnessed birth know this, too: The human baby is utterly dependent. Because of the abbreviated gestation, required by our big heads, we are biologically required to love our babies. We are only human because we can create community and care for one another. Our big heads can write symphonies; but they can also create nuclear bombs. Care is just as important as innovation.

The head came out, and along with it a deluge of liquids. I held the little body as it slid out into my arms, bloody and gasping for air. Like her parents. Like the whole world into which she'd come.

You've done this before.

My wife sat on the toilet and put the child to her breast. We cried at the bloody and awesome beauty. She was our beautiful, cosmic surprise. I had caught her, our unexpected third daughter.

This is how the universe works: We didn't know that we'd have three daughters, but the world is unimaginable without each of them. There is a perfection in this, a thing to listen to in the world. Their days are spent in a maelstrom of creative energy, creating, imagining, making worlds. *Three girls.* This is something in itself to listen to.

When I close my eyes, I see those drops of blood on my hands, like the raindrops falling into my hands on the Mozambican beach. To live in this world is to have blood on your hands;

to be alive is to have the courage not to turn away, because something is being birthed out of the bloody mess.

I caught her. Perhaps, one day, when I fall and fail in countless ways, she will catch me, too. For we spend so much of our lives trying to fly, trying to touch the sun. Trying to be like a god. But the real story always begins with a fall; the real story only begins with descent.

PART I
INFERNO

Salimmo suso, ei primo ed io secondo,
Tanto ch'io vidi delle cose belle
Che porta il ciel, per un pertugio tondo;
E quindi uscimmo a riveder le stelle.

—Dante, *Inferno*, Canto XXXIV, 136-139

1. BEGINNINGS
1973-1992

MY EARLIEST MEMORIES ARE OF THE VASTNESS, EMPTINESS, AND LONELINESS OF SPACE. As a young child, I am fascinated by the stars. I take classes at the planetarium. Each night, I ponder the immensity of the universe, and my own smallness in it. If the cosmos really is so great, and I so small, then ours must be an impossibly lonely world. I sleep in a small room adjacent to a larger playroom. Two doors separate me from my parents and brother. I am left to ponder the universe, my insomnia, the two doors, alone.

It is 1973. I'm born alongside the twins, hip hop and mass incarceration, who will follow us around throughout our lives. In this year, 1973, the US Department of Defense invents the "Global Positioning System," initiating our war against getting lost. I will spend my life lost, trying to find something; I will spend my life trying to get lost.

The Vietnam War ends, as Nixon leaves office, as the radicalism of the sixties begins its slow descent into self-indulgence, as the civil rights movement pretends to do the same. People are more concerned about the price of oil than about remaking the world. And then, as the 70s turns to the 80s, they focus on getting ahead. Being born in the 70s also means that I am born into a post-civil-rights America, and an America after the renewed immigration. It is a world, unlike that of my parents, in which I am exposed to different colors, each bringing its own concerns and worldview. At the same time, unlike my parents, I am born into a world of radical self-indulgence. I am expected to succeed only at success. Somehow, in ways no high priest ever explains to us, the world is going to work out based on this principle.

There is a city: Rochester, NY. It is the home my grandfather chose for his family, because it was fertile ground for the social gospel—the work to apply the social justice teachings of Jesus in the real world, the world of suffering and despair. He studies at the seminary there, then finds work in the streets, on skid row. We don't know it yet, but Rochester has begun its descent already.

But I live in a bubble. Unlike most of my parents' friends, we stay in the city, in a pleasant and isolated neighborhood called Browncroft. I have freedoms there that today's children only dream about. The summers stretch out forever, and we begin our days by wandering out into the streets to find other kids. The search lasts all day.

While Browncroft is a fine place to grow up in many ways, it is also limiting. I always feel that there was something more—something more exciting, more terrifying. Something that would make me feel alive. I can't find it in Browncroft.

We are taught that we could have it all—anything we desire—except for the only things we could really ever expect: living like a human being, and love.

We eat out of plastic and then put ourselves into plastic containers. Lines between happy meal and happy child become blurred. Should it be any surprise that the plastic generation—mine—gives birth to the social media generation? If you build a world out of plastic, it is only a matter of time before the soul becomes plastic, too. It will take some good drugs to get over that, and we take them all. We don't have Facebook to dull our senses.

We are free, American kids. We can come and go as we please, wander the streets, even in the dark, even when we are barely old enough to ride a bike. No one ever knows where we are or what we are doing. There is an undeniable beauty in this, an unrestrained joy that we feel. And, at the same time, we learn that the most essential—and therefore most ill-defined and unquestioned—American virtue, *freedom*, when taken to its extreme, becomes *loneliness*.

My father returns from the Vietnam war, bringing degrees and ambition and unprocessed scars he'll never talk about, to raise his family there. He has put whatever happened there away, deep inside, and focuses on his work. And so, he is seldom home, always working. And he's good at it. He builds success upon success in the office. Home, being a father, which requires more excavation than building, is more of a struggle. But in spite of this absence, he teaches me things: that there is virtue in taking care of one's family, in hard work; but most significantly, that there is shame in having any needs of one's own. My mother loves my brother and me, even if there's more competition than joy in the way we feel that love. She teaches me that I am smart and special, and I learn to value myself insofar as I can win and accomplish things. And so, I am raised in a home that is generous but joyless. I become this creature of post-war, white America: privileged and free—so free that I am alone.

This—my freedom and my loneliness—will one day lead me to leave for the ends of the Earth, where, paradoxically, it is revealed that the Earth is a circle.

There is a space—perhaps ten feet wide—behind our garage. There is a chain-link fence on the other side, and behind that some tangled bushes. On the side of the garage, there is also a space, about the same size, flanked by the garage of our next-door-neighbor—a shut-in whom I never remember even seeing by the name of Mrs Dinky. Since the absurdly-named and reclusive Mrs Dinky never ventures out, I have the run of both areas behind the garage. There, I dig holes in search of dinosaur bones and treasure. I build forts. There, I can be alone, away from the demons and from the taunts of other children. There, I can find my first adventures and get my hands dirty. I keep digging, day after day. There are things, I know already, that you can only find by digging.

When my brother is born, it doesn't make me very happy. Many times, I will hear the painful story of tackling my mother when she comes home from the hospital with the little blond boy. Matt is round and fair and seeks out the approval of his elders; I am olive-skinned, stocky and athletically built, and care little about what anyone thinks. "The boy is five years old and a goddamn expert on everything," my father says.

Matt and I fight fiercely, and my mother is left to deal with it, for our father works obscene hours. We rarely see him. When I've finished fighting my brother, and my dad finally does show up, I fight him, too. My mother watches quietly.

There are also many times when we, like all brothers, are one another's sole companion and playmate. I occasionally will come to sleep in his room—"a sleepover"—on the floor at the foot of his bed. These times fade into memory as we grow older and apart. At the same time, they become the eternity we've made as children, a part of us, even as men. Childhood is a maker of eternities. Once, when I am much older— perhaps twelve or thirteen—I go on a trip to a cabin with some friends. On the second day, I receive a phone call. It is my father. My brother has been hit by a car. He will be okay, but his leg is badly broken. I lie awake that night, thinking of my brother, who is no longer sleeping next to me.

There is a school, sprawling and industrial, only a mile from my home but a world away. It is around this time that I would decide to attend East High School, a decision that will plunge me into a world beyond the Browncroft bubble. It is a choice that I embrace; for it gives me the new worlds to explore that I've been seeking. But it is a chaotic place. Like most big public schools, it isn't nurturing or safe. When the time comes for my brother to go to high school, he decides on Catholic school. Our paths diverge. His question and mine will be different.

I proceed through school and into what we call junior high school, a star in the little world of CYO basketball. A lonely child whose only joy is the basketball court, whose days are spent pondering deep mysteries that I share with no one, my dream is to play in the NBA. My parents had given me the option of Catholic school, but I chose, and I would frequently do throughout my life, the path of difference and difficulty. I want something harder and different from the cold and joyless life I'd been given. East, at the time, is called a "junior-senior high school"; many of its students, like me, essentially begin high school as seventh graders. As ill-conceived an idea as this might be, it opens up worlds for me that have never been available in the prison of Browncroft and of the single classroom in which I've felt trapped.

I've already become aware of my privilege, an awareness that will pain me throughout my time at East—I, the son of the lawyer, in school with the impoverished sons and daughters of slavery and Jim Crow and flights from oppression abroad. I go to East High School in part because it seems unjust to go to a private school simply because my parents can afford it.

The 80s is a decade marked by self-absorption, by the cult of wealth and its sister, violence. Crack comes to Rochester as it does to other cities around this time. East High is home to emerging drug dealers and to the sons and daughters of what we call "geekers"—those addicted to the drug. Sometimes the dealers and the addicts come from the same families, live under the same roofs.

East High School, its sports teams absurdly and racistly named "The Orientals", is known for being a somewhat troubled school with an excellent basketball program—our white competitors, less complicated in their racism, mock us with signs saying "funny, they don't look oriental"—and if you are smart enough or white enough to get into the honors program in its quasi-segregated system, you can actually get a good education. I'm not especially interested in getting an education, only in basketball and in pushing the boundaries of the little worlds in which I've been imprisoned. I want to ask questions, or at least to discover them, but I have no idea what questions even to ask.

There is a hotel downtown, once luxurious but now, like the rest of the city, seedy and falling into disrepair.

I get a skateboard. My buddy Danny and I buy them together. We've seen the other kids in the neighborhood—cooler kids than us—skating, and we want that juice. So we buy the skateboards and start to hang with other skaters. These kids seem older, more streetwise than us. We are connected now to subcultures of rebellion—some good, some bad. Racist skinheads linger at the fringes. We know about them, but don't know them. We hear about them beating up gays in the park where they went to meet up with other men.

These are the days of street skating. Urban youth like us roam the city streets, ostensibly looking for a railing to grind or a ledge to jump, but really looking for the freedom of the streets. We can go anywhere in our little, decaying city of abandoned lots and factories, subway tunnels and alleys. We fall down and bleed, and that's the point, because feeling something is what we've been trained not to do, and while we think we rebel against signs that ban skating on sidewalks, it's really the numbing that we rebel against.

Patrick, whom I've known since pre-school, skates too. We spend hours wandering the city, often just finding a place to sit and talk—or talk shit. This is what we do. We talk about sex, even though we've never had it. We insult each other homophobically, hoping we don't turn out to be gay because we understand this as the worst thing that could happen to us. We might make jokes about AIDS, too, because we know then it is a "gay disease."

We don't know that people are dying in the 80s of AIDS simply because no one cares about a "gay disease" and just how unfunny that is.

We skate past the Cadillac Hotel each day, that once-grand, downtown establishment occupied by the city's castaways. We know not to stop there. But we don't know that Patrick's father sometimes stays there.

We know vaguely that Patrick's father isn't around like he used to be, but don't know that he's gay and that he's left the family now for someone else—looking, like us perhaps, for something he's never been told he could have—that he was staying for a time in that very hotel, that he could have been one of those men in the park. Like my father, he has unanswered questions that are never asked out loud. We know none of this, because we are boys, and ashamed and unable to communicate, even if we are sitting and talking in alleys and parking lots for hours and hours, day after day. I won't know, until years later, or really understand, when I learn that his father dies of AIDS, even then only relayed in a whisper from the embarrassed elders.

I meet Antonio in study hall in the eighth grade. He just sort of starts talking to me then, and one way of looking at it would be to say that the conversation will continue for decades.

The teacher tells everyone to sit down and take out some work.

"You know they don't really care," he says. Antonio is sitting across from me, a smirk on his face. "They don't care if we do our work. They really just looking for a reason to kick us out."

"Of study hall?" I ask.

"Well, yeah—at first. Then they'll kick us out of school."

I nod. I smile. I am pleased at how easily he includes me in his "us". Antonio continues. "You see, these teachers don't really give a fuck about us Black kids."

I nod again.

"Hey, Ton'!" someone yells from across the room. "Explain this to the whiteboy: Tell him why you always got something to say about the white man but you always chasing after his woman. Jungle-fever-ass-nigga."

Everyone laughs. Antonio smiles. He self-consciously dresses like a nerd, wears clothes that are not at all in fashion, as part of a calculated effort to craft himself as the Black Intellectual. He *is* an intellectual, in spite of his lack of education, but he is also from the streets, and everyone knows it. He is no "bougie nigga from the suburbs", as people sometimes try to claim. He is always ready for a fight—a verbal one, anyway. This guy is going after what some would consider his weak point—his well-known interest in white girls.

"I'm a brother," he answers. "Not a nigger. And why should I *not* be with a white woman. What? You think they too good for us?"

His adversary was momentarily silenced. "Besides," Antonio continues. "*They* chase after *me*."

Everyone laughs, including me.

East High exposes me to new worlds. While most of its population is Black, there is a large number of Puerto Ricans, as well as immigrant children from all over the world. I come to know Jamaicans and Haitians, Panamanians and Mexicans, Eritreans and Kenyans, Laotians and Vietnamese, Portuguese and Greeks. But the dominant culture is post–civil rights-era, urban, poor, and Black. It is a school culture dominated by the violence of urban America and the emergence of Hip Hop. My classmates come to school with guns and flashy new cars; they come angry because they have no money to eat, come angry because their mothers are addicts or their fathers are incarcerated.

The school, like other large urban schools, is run with industrial efficiency and a prison-like mentality. The security guards, called sentries, implore us not to be late as we march the halls. Fights—usually between girls—are commonplace. But the feeling, most of the day, for the many years I spend the majority of my time there, is of *joy*. Everyone is laughing. There is music and dancing. There is conversation and debate. Like most adolescents, I think that the playful exuberance of my generation means something new, means that we, somehow, will not be subject to becoming cynical or, worse, boring. But these kids are doing what their ancestors have always done: They make art to process the despair. In 1989, we are taught to worship success; failures are our own fault. We have no movement, no community, nothing to fight for. In Black America, there is Hip Hop, an artistic movement based on the rhythm of the urban American ghetto.

I soak it all in. I want to be a part of this strange, new world.

We start to drink. Alcohol makes us feel free—perhaps it is the risk of it, the illicitness, perhaps just the chemical transformation. Either way, it is transformative, and that's what I am looking for.

One weekend, Patrick is watching his neighbor's dogs while they are out of town, and they have a full bar, so we go over one night to sample it. We sip a variety of liquors, mixing them grotesquely with whatever sweet shit we find. After getting a nice buzz, we leave for my house to play video games.

Danny starts acting silly on the way home. It gets to the point where it's just ridiculous and annoying, and we tell him to shut up and to stop pretending he's drunk.

But he keeps it up all the way home. He passes out on the couch while Patrick and I play Super Mario Brothers.

After a while we turn around and realize he's sleeping in a pool of his own vomit. *Oh shit*. I tell my parents there's something wrong with him, that he must be sick. They call his father.

"Has he been drinking?"

Not that we know of.

"He's drunk."

We don't know anything about that.

They take him to the hospital to get his stomach pumped. Patrick and I deny any knowledge of his drinking for decades after the episode.

Weed comes next, after my parents move into a big house and give me the attic room. We get high and drunk just about every night, listening to *De La Soul is Dead*.

No longer the star of CYO, I have to learn to play street ball, the way they play at East High, where basketball is a game for the people. Unlike football, based upon militarism and without any individual creativity, basketball is about finding freedom and space within confined spaces. It is about expressing oneself in an arbitrarily restricted context. Those who praise teamwork without creativity, who say that the game is only about the most useful means of victory, do not understand this sport—and many others—at all. For basketball would not exist—no one would even care!—if not for those who express themselves, even when, at times, this expression costs the team. Here is how it feels: there is a rhythm to the game.

The dribble. You cannot really understand the game, or even play it, until you can actually feel the rhythm of the dribble, until you find yourself, full speed, leading a fast break, opponent backpedaling and at your mercy. The dribble, the rhythm, is the game. It is whence all creativity, all meaning, all substance, comes. Those who say it is a big man's game don't understand it either. It would be nothing without the dribble, the provenance of the little man. And the one thing I would learn to do was dribble. It was my first contribution to the creation of a new world, of finding freedom in confined space through creativity.

When the weather is warm, I ride my bike each day up to Cobbs Hill Park. It is close to home but a million miles away. Cobbs Hill is one the primary outdoor courts in Rochester. There is a specific hierarchy and there are specific rules I have to learn. The oldtimers run the courts, and, just as significantly, the conversations outside the courts. It is best to ask them if you want to play. They could be harsh, but also generous. They are far more likely to give a young boy like me a chance than one of the serious ballers, grown men in their prime, who are the true stars of the court. The oldtimers have developed games and personalities to deal with their physical limitations in comparison to the younger men, who sometimes are playing at the college level during the winter.

Charlie is the mayor and chief counsel of the Cobbs Hill courts. He will leave me more memories of his voice than his game, except that he has a sort of classic, old-man, back-to-the-basket guard's game, backing his man down into the high post, then finding an open man, only occasionally taking a fade-away. But he is kind to me: "He's only a young boy," he tells another man who is getting on me about my mistakes on the court.

"Banana" is an oldtimer I often speak to. He is less of a personality off the court, but more of a star on it. Having lost much of his quickness ("washed up" is whispered from time to time) he still has the mind of a point guard. I like him and his game and study what he does. He is sensitive about his game and, in a world where a quick retort to any insult is the norm, he grows sullen and quiet if someone taunts him. "I may not be as fast as you," he tells me, "may not be able to shoot as good. I may not have read as many books. But I know what it's like to be 35 years old. You don't know nothing about that." He is right.

But I *am* fast and I *can* shoot. I am growing to be strong and fast, ready to do battle in the world of men and boys.

"Get on the line, you *fatheads*."

Gym class at East consists primarily of standing on a line in order to be counted, being called a variety of names—"fathead" being the least vulgar in their repertoire—by the gym teachers, and playing basketball. One of the major decisions I will later recall making at this point in my life is whether or not I want to get sweaty that day.

"Are you a bunch of fucking fairies?" Mr. Chilton, the portly, toupeed man who coaches the football team, is the most vulgar of them all. "Get on the fucking line!" He is yelling at the "non-swimmers" who, to his unending exasperation, seem incapable of standing on a line in order to be counted. The class is stratified in a way that mirrors society: The swimmers, by far the smallest group, are mostly white and middle class; the middle group are people who could swim a little, the upwardly mobile; and the non-swimmers are the masses, those who, according to the gym teachers, would "sink like a stone". In spite of the emphasis on swimming groups, we rarely swim.

"I'm getting tired of being nice to people." Antonio is most expansive and, in some ways, generous with himself, when he is angry. "These white motherfuckers—I mean, you're cool, I'm not referring you here—these white motherfuckers really don't care about me at all. They pretend to be your friend, but…" And so continues the dialogue that will span decades.

East High brings a chaos that can't be escaped. A kid can either embrace it, revel in it, or be swallowed by it.

I am an embracer.

I learn how to skip class, sometimes escaping through a back door out into the world's boundless freedom, other times spending extra time in the lunchroom. One never knows what to expect there. One day a fight, another a stink bomb is set off, another a massive food fight. Rather than apply my intelligence to my studies, I learn to work the system: I discover that if you don't ever show up to a particular class, it will never be recorded and you could have a free period without consequence.

School is easy. My grades rarely suffer. Classes themselves are often a party anyway. There are Spanish classes taught by long-term substitutes who know no Spanish. It is in Spanish class that I meet Fatima, her father a Black Nationalist, a Nation-of-Islam-Muslim who lives in Florida, her mother Puerto Rican.

I arrive at her house one night to pick her up to go to a party. Their mom offers me a beer and casually chats. I am a teenager and can't believe how easy this is going to be, can't believe I'm not being asked any hard questions. But her older sister, Amira, is there, waiting. *What is your intension with my sister?* She asks. I am momentarily stunned by her intensity. I know her from school, but not well—she dates my friend Ronnie from the basketball team, Ronnie who was always smiling and could jump out of the gym. Her little sister, Denise, perhaps three at the time, is there, too. She seems apart from her sisters in a way I cannot place. A different father, yes, but it has more to do with timing. The family was already moving constantly by the time Denise was born. The structure that existed for the older children is absent, and she is raised by committee.

Our eyes meet and she runs to me and gives me a hug. I am now on the committee. I pick her up and toss her in the air. It is the thing I will do from now on, every time we meet. I disarm Amira with my kindness to the little sister, with a few jokes. Fatima and I are off. We get drunk on the way to a party. She kisses me, then passes out. My friends try to sexually assault her. I stop them, but don't stop being friends with them.

Amira is the oldest and the little mother of the family. From the day their father left, she has cared for her younger sisters. There is a strength in her that is incomprehensible to me. I love them—Denise, Amira, and Fatima. They are alive in a way that I have not yet been. And I begin to connect to something that will allow me to feel deeply—and feeling is what I crave more than anything—while being safe from the vulnerability that I've been taught to fear. Denise, without a father, abused and confused, begins to *need* me. And I love this feeling, that someone needs me. In time, Amira and I, sharing this need, become the best of friends.

In this way, I come to fall in love with Fatima. It is a falling that has more to do with my own need to be alive, and to be needed, than anything else. But, as is often the case for boys entering into manhood, it becomes intensely personal. She is at once kind and cruel, brilliant and ignorant. We are hardly ready for anything close to the intensity of it all, but this is usually the way when kids fall in love.

We're from Lewis Street
Mighty, Might Lewis Street
Everywhere we go
People want to know
Who we are, so we tell them
We're from Lewis Street
Might, Mighty Lewis Street...

—Camp Song, Lewis Street Center, 1992

There is a community center in the heart of one of Rochester's poorest neighborhoods. Lewis Street is a remnant of an old system of "settlement houses", still in place in Rochester. The idea was to create a center in a poor community where middle class people can come and educate the poor on how to not be poor. It is debatable how effective this is for the poor people; for the rich, it certainly beats giving all your money away.

I have to get a job for the summer before I go to college. This is what they tell me. I know nothing about jobs or how one might find one. I've really only done odd jobs, some babysitting or lawn mowing. Amira's and Fatima's mother works at Lewis Street. She tells me I can work there. I like kids, so this seems like a good idea.

By the time I get there, Rochester's middle class is mostly focused on staying as far away as possible from poor people. Lewis Street Center's Summer Camp is run by the people who live in or near the community. I am the only exception.

The camp is staffed primarily by old women, usually unemployed the rest of the year, and the neighborhood drug dealers. The drug dealers, generally, make better counselors. The fact that they come home and sell drugs to the parents of the campers seems to trouble no one—or at least seems so entrenched in the way things are that no one really brings it up. They aren't villains, this is clear. They are trapped in the same cycles as the addicts. Some even sell to their parents.

Every day after work I go to the basketball courts, then I return to Amira's apartment on Clinton Avenue—she is on her own now. It is a little, dingy place, hot as hell in the summer and without much in the way of windows, surrounded by concrete. There is a house that has been converted into apartments, out of which drugs are sold, across the lot. It isn't clear whose lot it is, for pretty much anyone could park there. I pull into that lot one day and am immediately surrounded, blocked in by the police. Some come in regular cop cars, others in the undercover dick cars. The undercover cops wear ski masks to hide their identity. They spring from the cars and run across the lot to the apartment house and begin to barge their way in, like Grinches stealing Christmas. I stand watching as they walk sadly away. What and who they've looked for is no longer there.

I go in the house to tell Fatima and Amira what I've seen. They give me smiles, the sort of smiles I hate, about a whiteboy getting a taste of ghetto life. I ignore it. Ronnie, Amira's boyfriend and my basketball teammate, comes over and asks if I want to make a run with him. "You should stay," says Fatima. "Amira wants Ronnie to stay and maybe he won't go if you don't."

"I'll be back soon," I say, sort of believing it.

We spend the next five hours driving around the city, chasing women (mostly Ronnie) and getting drunk (mostly me). I return to the obligatory argument, which spreads out across the days of the summer and into the months and years of past hurts. The little apartment barely has enough room for happy people, much less two arguing couples. We move out into the parking lot, now empty of police, concluding with my kicking my forty ounces of beer across the pavement. When the rage has been exhausted, we all sleep fitfully as M, Amira's baby, coos away in his crib.

I wake up every morning in an exhausted haze of marijuana smoke and cheap beer and bitterness to get ready for work at Lewis Street, where I am put in charge of a group of kindergarteners and find there that I had a gift with children. I am ready for new things but don't know enough to know what they are.

The course of my life, like the broader course of the civilization into which I am born, is one of apocalypse, of planetary polycrisis. The roots of civilizational crisis, as for an individual, can often be found in the depths, before we were even aware that anything was wrong.

We didn't know it when I was born, but the seeds had already been planted. It's more than just climate change. The world is on fire. Borders teeming with migrants fleeing the interconnected web of geopolitical, economic, and ecological collapse. Billionaires squeezing every last penny from a system that cannot be sustained. There is a deepening sense of unease, unmooring—the inner climate unravels with the outer. And this is because there was something in the system that happened long ago, unseen and unconscious, that already carried with it the seeds of the crisis.

We are living in a global civilization based upon the values and worldview of capitalism. The idea is a simple one, an idea that runs counter to every culture that came before it: We are fundamentally individuals, in competition with one another. And from this we have created crisis upon crisis. We seek to solve these crises with more of the same: technology and engineering, drugs and screens. All of it is rooted in the central cosmological fact, that we are individuals, alone in a universe that we must control, conquer, own.

I will learn this the hard way. I will learn that my own deepest fears and anxieties were more than personal, but also a part of a broader cultural trend that taught me these values.

The apocalypse is more than the destruction of our physical world. We are watching systems unravel because a worldview is unraveling. When taken to the furthest logical extreme, a worldview rooted in independence takes us ultimately to loneliness. And not merely a feeling of being alone, but a deeper, cosmic loneliness, a singularity of sorts—the apocalypse. The story we've been told—that the world is something to buy and own; that we are essentially individuals, alone and lonely—doesn't hold. Things are falling apart.

It's tempting to offer the reader something more prescriptive. Perhaps a list of solutions or practices. I am not suggesting we ought not do anything. But I am suggesting that to do something that still sees us as acting as an individual rather than entangled in an interconnected world, traps us in the same apocalypse. This is what happens when we teach our children how to fix the crisis but not about the relationships and values and beliefs that got us here in the first place. Even collective actions that do not account for our descent into the depths of the soul and looking honestly and courageously at our own wounds does not allow us to confront the shadow that often leads us to avoid our own participation in the crisis.

We have to descend.

And what does this mean? In order to reimagine the story we've told about who we are and our place in the cosmos, we must go to the depths, look within. This requires a poetic engagement with the world. There is a reason that the fascists always come after the poets. We must feel the world—its texture, its depth, its brokenness and its beauty. For the whole problem is that we've tried to remove its depth, to turn it into product and us into consumer. The world has been flattened, paved over. It's lost its wildness. Indeed, we've paved over the wildness in ourselves, too. And so, while I work to make things whole, I also will become aware that I must excavate the brokenness of my youth, to feel the world, in order to discover a new life. In order to fall in love.

After the summer of '92, I leave Rochester for Chicago. All I've ever wanted is to fall in love. This is the surest way to become a human being, and, as a boy, I have always felt like something less than human. Less than a man. I know that somehow I have to find a way to become one, but have no idea how. I don't know then that manhood means passing through a birth canal, being burned by the fire of love, being nearly drowned in the oceanic depth of soul and world. I know that I have to discover myself, somehow, in the world beyond, which is really only another name for myself, if only I can see the depth, the texture of the world. I start in Chicago.

2. ALTAMIRA
1995

CHICAGO, AND THE WORLD, TURNS OUT TO BE so much bigger than I've ever imagined. I arrive there thinking I know something about the world. Of course I know very little. On my first visit home I look out the window of the plane and see downtown, once so splendorous, and see what looks like a little factory in the middle of nowhere. It turns out to be Rochester, shrunken by the immensity of Chicago. There is a whole world beyond Rochester, and I have come to Chicago to find it.

The Chicago I find at first isn't really Chicago at all, but the *University of* Chicago. Somehow, I get in, in spite of my general disinterest in all things academic, to this famous institution. I sit in the shadow of Rockefeller and Freidman, study Kant and Plato, and barely know who any of them are. My early days are focused on basketball, on drinking beer, and on trying to avoid being found out—trying to avoid letting them know that I am really not an intellectual at all, that I've never even written much of anything, never read much of what I am supposed to have read.

It is good for me to come to Chicago. Nowhere else could I learn so much about America. It is the black-and-white-est of cities. And what is more American than that? I am shocked at first at the segregation, nothing like I've ever seen in Rochester, where at least the ethnic minorities live together. Here, in Chicago, not only is there segregation between white and Black, but also between Puerto Rican and Mexican, Irish and Italian.

Regularly, I pass by a statue on Ellis Avenue celebrating the creation, there, in the depths of what were then athletic facilities (it is now the library), of the atomic bomb. It is something that could only be celebrated in such an atomized, compartmentalized world. An achievement of the human mind over human compassion and good sense. What I am not taught is that the narrative of the human brain being our only and greatest asset was false: We were born in Africa, the ape with a big head, containing a big brain. Our brains were so big, in fact, that we were born premature and helpless. The human brain necessitated a further evolution of mammalian compassion: we were not only human because of our big-headedness, but because of our big-heartedness, too.

I pass by the absurd, deliberately abstract statue—there are no incinerated Japanese children beneath—on a dismal and frozen day, marveling at this macabre celebration. At U of C, they wear T-shirts making fun of the Chicago weather and the misery/brainyness of the student body: "Hell Does Freeze Over". An homage to the lowest circle of Dante's inferno: Ice.

"Now I become death, destroyer of worlds." Oppenheimer is said to have stated this at the nuclear test site in New Mexico, quoting the *Bhagavad Gita*. They had just conducted a test that no one could say with certainty would not, in fact, destroy our world. It still may. But in these dark days in my first year at the University of Chicago, it does seem the world is ending. Not so much because of the possibility of atomic bombs, but because of the inevitability of our atomized lives. We do not yet know how lonely we can get.

It is also a shock to me how different the basketball culture is at The University of Chicago from what I've become used to. I haven't played with so many whiteboys since my CYO days. I have to unlearn all that I've learned at East High and Cobbs Hill. But I am fast and can dribble and shoot. I dominate the early pickup games. The guys on the team like me and respect my game. It is strange, though. These are guys from suburban Middle America. Republicans, mostly. The athletic culture, even at The University of Chicago, somehow manages to remain apart from the deeper, intellectual culture of the institution.

Something else happens that's strange: when practice begins, I realize that the coaches have no interest in me. Relegated to the bench, often in street clothes, I never play a minute in my depressing freshman year.

My initial excitement at the intellectual opportunities, the parties, and the pure freedom of college life wanes as the seasons change. The gray skies loom day after bittercold day, seeming to blend in with the neo-gothic architecture. The gargoyles taunt me from above. My girlfriend leaves me. My grades, which initially were quite good, suffer.

Depressed, I get on a train back to Rochester to see what I can salvage of my relationship. There is something sad about train stations. They require a full commitment of the journey; there is a pain inherent in them, a knowing that one is going somewhere far and that it may be a long time before one returns. The train passes through the night. I sit sleeplessly and try to sleep, try to write. There is nothing but sentimental bullshit, nothing but adolescent melodrama. Outside, only Blackness. I can only see my own reflection.

There, in Rochester, I find only more gray. She has a new boyfriend. I wander the streets of Rochester, those empty, post-industrial streets I'd once roamed on my skateboard, for a whole night. I return to Chicago that spring, lift weights, practice my jump shot, get drunk nearly every night, and get terrible grades. My professors are cold and arrogant, even as the Chicago springtime slowly awakes.

We thought—both of us—that my love was something unique, something superhuman. But it wasn't. I had a choice then: recede or confront the world in its fullness and its finitude, its beauty and its ugliness, a confrontation that brought with it the greatest of all risks: being born and falling in love. Again.

I am still digging. Without any conscious self-awareness of the fact, the little boy who used to dig behind the garage comes into the first inklings of manhood, of selfhood, by digging.

The archaeological process is actually so simple that it is absurd: the deeper one digs, the further into the past one goes. And the more universally shared the past will be. The surface may contain a shared past of a people, whereas if one goes deeper one might find something shared among all people. Still deeper one might find the story of all animals, or all life, or even geological stories, shared by the entire planet.

It is possible to travel the world and never get below the surface. How many of us have gotten on planes and flown from one, sterile, Westernized city to another, thinking we saw something of significance? The trick is to find both depth and breadth. At least then it was possible to get lost, to get away from the screen, to be forced to confront oneself. This is what happens in the depths of the cave, what happens when I decide that the only way to dig deep is to travel far.

I've never been anywhere before—only some family vacations—so I take with me an absurd amount of stuff: an enormous bag that seems like it was made for transporting dead bodies, containing most of my worldly possessions, for I have nowhere to store my things during the summer break from the dorms. I bring my whole self with me: this is what it means to be a traveler. The tourist can leave behind a job, a family, a life. But the traveler is *there*. I don't know this yet. Don't even know what it means to be a self. Or whole.

I have come from Chicago, from the University of Chicago, more specifically, as part of a program to work at a Paleolithic dig in northern Spain. Dig for a month, get three "A's, I am told. At the University of Chicago, this seems like a good deal.

I come to Spain from Rochester, too. This is the first summer I'm not going home, the first summer of my manhood. Or perhaps the summer in which I began to inch my way toward becoming a man.

My first couple of years in Chicago have been lived out in two places: pieces of me in Rochester, pieces in Chicago. I haven't been to enough places yet to know that this is how we live. Pieces of us left behind everywhere we've been, gifts for those we've known.

I arrive then, in Spain, knowing little of the world beyond urban America, wondering what it means to be a man—or a human being at all—and yearning to be alive. There is a guy I know a little, Mike Silva, who is also going on the trip, and we've decided to meet up in Madrid and find our way to Santander in the north.

Mike is a baseball player from a family of Providence fisherman. Something has happened to him; it's clear. He is a great storyteller; but all his stories seem to be avoiding the heart of the matter, whatever has happened that's made him so sad and bitter. He is a working class kid at an elite school, and wears this identity proudly—some of it is this. But there seems to be something more.

I get off the plane in Madrid, retrieve my ridiculously-large-body-bag, and wander out onto the Spanish street. Never having been abroad, I really don't know enough to know how lost I might be. I fully expect not to connect with Mike. To my surprise, there he is, grinning at me and helping me get my bag.

"What the fuck is in this bag?"

I smile. "Well, you know. All my stuff."

"Jesus fucking Christ."

We jump on a bus and Mike leads me to the hostel he's found. Two beds and a shared bathroom for a mere 100 pesetas a night.

I'm jetlagged and hung over. I got drunk on the plane, thinking this would be a good way to fall asleep. But Mike is ready to show me this world he's already discovered. And so, I discover the Spanish night. This is Old Spain, the Spain of Franco and Hemingway. It hasn't quite fully even joined Europe, much less the global economy. These are the in-between days in Spain: free from Francoism, but not yet inundated with American culture, not yet an EU cosmopolis filled with eastern European and African immigrants. The Spanish night offers itself to a twenty year old from America like a window into the past; and, unable to see the future before us, we do not even realize how far away that past really was.

We begin with food—a *bocadillo* and some *tapas*. And wine and sangria. *Cuba libre* and *calimocho*. Drinks are poured and walked out into the streets. The Streets! In Spain, there is still such a thing as the street, a public space so lost to the children—as we were—of America in the 80s that we haven't even realized we've missed it.

The nights pour forth deep into mornings. Days are spent sleeping. Mike and I visit museums. I never bore of the Spanish night, or of the tricks the painters at the old churches and museums played with light. But Mike begins to miss "the States".

"Let's go north," he says, looking for something else, as I will later come to see, he always will. We hop on a train heading to Santander, the closest city to where we'd be staying to work the dig.

Mike tells me about how he came to Chicago as we sit in our shared room in Santander. A few years before, he left Providence, where he played Division I baseball, and transferred to Chicago. He is good enough in school to get in, but the intellectual climate never really suits him. He misses his family—all fishermen going back several generations—and his buddies in Providence. But there is a girl.

Before the baseball season even starts, Mike blows out his knee. Then he begins to make certain discoveries about his girlfriend. It isn't so much that she's cheated on him. It was more like she was some kind of a sex addict. She's been with hundreds of men, she eventually confesses, after he tearfully confronts her when he discovers he has herpes.

Unable to work out because of his knee, Mike puts on weight. He starts going bald. The dark and cold winter spreads out before him like an abyss. Chicago is no place for the depressed.

But even here, in Sunny Spain, Hemingway's playground, Mike can find no joy. As we drink the nights away, he grows more and more sullen as I fall in love with Old Spain, a dying place that I am too young and foolish to even see is disappearing before my eyes.

By the time we make our way to the old Jesuit Seminary where we are to stay, Mike's cynicism has reached a fever pitch. As uninspired as he is by Europe, he is even less enamored with academia. He rants about "punitive measures" taken by the faculty. "Typical academic bullshit" is the oft-repeated description of everything from the classes we take to the schedule to the food.

He has a friend from Providence, Kate, who is a student-assistant on the trip. Kate is a Black girl who's been adopted by a white family who mostly spends her time at the University of Chicago around a group of Koreans. In fact, she even looks slightly Asian and wonders whether or not she is partly Korean.

To Mike's further dismay and unspoken, subtle, unconscious jealousy, Kate and I strike up a summer romance. I am too immature to see that it is a good thing. Perhaps I am afraid, later, that if I continue the relationship beyond Spain it will lose something of its allure. So I will leave it there.

Archeology is not as glamorous as one raised on Indiana Jones might think. Day after day brushing away millennia of dust and picking through the garbage of our ancestors. Shell fragments and bone chips. Rocks that may have been used as tools. The imagination of the digger is far more interesting than the digging itself: These were people, millennia ago, no different from us, really, but for thousands of years of culture. They lived from what they could kill and find, inseparable from the land, its plants, animals and patterns of weather. They were the same as us, and yet different in almost every way.

One day, we are told that we are visiting the nearby cave called *Altamira* for the day, so we take a brief ride to the nearby cave in our Land Rovers. It is so close to our cave—I imagine that our professor is jealous of its discoverers, stuck as he is with this crap cave of little bits of garbage. It is closed to the public, but the professor gets us in.

I have never heard of *Altamira* before this day, have no idea what it is. I have never heard, for example, that Picasso once remarked that everything since those works was mere "decadence". I walk into its depths, led by a guide, not knowing what to expect. Perhaps, in my ignorance, I am no different from the others who've come, either the contemporaries of the artist-shamans who created them or later visitors who stumbled upon them. Having spent weeks in a cave already, I am uninspired by the solemn walk into its depths. But then, there they are. They move. The prey and the predator, dancing before me on the ceiling. Could these have been created by men or women so many thousands of years ago? Could this be the work of cave people, wandering about in animal skins?

In truth, those who created those images were at once no different—biologically, intellectually—from me, and yet they were as different as one could possibly imagine. They were embedded in their world.

I will learn this many years later. I will learn that these are the things that make us human: experiencing the world as our womb and creating new worlds through symbol and story.

This world in which they painted was our world, too. It was a world of uncertainty, of humans encountering and decimating new species as they expanded. It was a world that was at once the same and entirely different from our own. For the first time, it was a world that was made by a creature—the human—through symbol.

They made handprints on the walls of the cave because they saw this as the womb of the Earth. They saw that to live meant to touch the edge of the world itself, the world that is our womb. They understood that to know themselves required going to the depths. They created art to fulfill a need no different from our own: because they were human.

What's more, the images within the cave were images of the stars. They were, like the human soul, both womb and nighttime sky, at once the within and the beyond of the self and world. They offer me an answer to the question of my earliest consciousness: how is it possible to not be alone in this vast and empty world?

These cave people were—in a very different way, it is true—just blinking into consciousness. This is Spain, in 1995. It is still Old Spain, but only just. Many more educated and worldly than me will see that something new is emerging, a new world in which there is no Spain, no womb at all, nothing in which to be embedded. I will also learn, years later, that the cave people have much to teach us. We can't go back the caves, completely. But we can remember, at least, to re-embed, to create, and touch the edge of our womb world.

Millennia ago, these people did something else, too: they encountered the edge of their world. The end of their world. Perhaps it took millennia more for that end/beginning to come forth. But it would. Their art both reflected and precipitated the ancient apocalypse. It is possible that it spoke to an apocalypse that is still happening. I know nothing of it in 1995. I know only that I need, like our ancient ancestors, to reach out toward the edge. I've been abroad, and I know that something felt alive in me as never before, as if it is not rootedness that made me real, but movement. I do not know then that I've never been rooted, and know nothing of what it would even mean.

3. CHILDREN'S CENTER #1
1995-1996

A FEW WEEKS AFTER QUITTING THE BASKETBALL TEAM DURING MY JUNIOR YEAR AT THE UNIVERSITY OF CHICAGO (after a sophomore season in which I play a lot, philosophical differences with the coaching staff finally come to a head) I find myself in a pickup game at the field house, fighting over a ball screen set by a 60-year-old woman. Normally, fighting over a ball screen requires a pretty significant amount of physicality. But what can I do? She is sixty years old, or thereabouts. She can't really play, but has nonetheless joined a game with men—most ranging from twenty to forty years younger—and has been barking orders at everyone throughout the game. As she sets the screen, I just stop. I look around. *What the fuck am I doing with my life?* I think.

After the game, she approaches me. She likes the way I play, she tells me. She asks me what I study, and is surprised to learn that I am an undergraduate. She asks me if I'd like to come work with her kids. "We play a lot of basketball," she explains.

A few days later, I show up at the Sue Duncan Children's Center, known to all as "Sue." It is always unclear if a person is talking about Sue the person or the place. It never matters; it's always both. We read a book with some kids then go up to the gym. When we come back down, we sit in a circle and she asks, to everyone and no one, explicitly to the children but secretly, unconsciously, to me: "What kind of life do you want to have?"

She hires me on the spot.

Sue is the disciplinarian—of parents and children alike. She believes, somehow, that if she could just create the correct system of rules, she could gain some control over a cruel and chaotic world.

We are in a church basement, decaying and rundown, like the Church as a whole. Water pours into the coatroom when it rains. Heat is inconsistent in winter. The floorboards in the gym are coming up.

Family—not religion or country—is the foundation of Sue's cosmos. And this gives the center its strength. For people come by the family. Usually, the children lead. The older ones wander in, younger in tow, sometimes in groups as large as eight or nine. They come for various reasons: because they love the little ones and want to find a safe place for them; because they want to learn; because they are bored or want friendship. These reasons are unarticulated. The young bring the old: aunties, mothers, grandmothers. Usually women, but not always.

In time, a family becomes a part of the community. Cousins and friends arrive. In time, generations flow; children become adults and have their own children, who will then come. It is an educational program, yes. But it is unlike anything else you could imagine. For Sue understands this one thing: that education, real education, can only happen in community.

Patricia is a relative newcomer to Sue. As is often the case, her children came first. Like many, they are angry and hurt and traumatized. Patricia was an addict. Sue sent her to rehab, and she has come back looking to re-imagine herself.

The mothers come to read with their children. Patricia quickly emerges as a leader among them. She has a big voice and a big personality. A natural leader. The kids call to her now on the street. She knows them all. When she hollers, everyone gets in line. The room where the little kids are read to soon becomes known as "Patricia's room."

For some parents, spending time with children isn't so easy. Marsha Jones has come from a family in which street life dominates. She's just buried a son who's been murdered on the streets of Chicago. Her decrepit husband, who, in his youth, had rank, I am told, in the El Rukn street gang, does little to help at home. As foul-mouthed as my high school gym teachers, Marsha has little patience for reading with her children. Still, she has a big heart and is smart, which she's passed on to her children. We decide that her best role is to sit by the door, letting people in. I call her "security". She spends her time reading cheap romance novels.

Marsha brings her own kids and other family members she's taken in. Once, one of her older sons returns from prison with the teenaged daughter of the woman he's started dating in prison. His girlfriend is now incarcerated. Left in charge of her daughter and not really knowing what to do, he comes back to Chicago to live with Marsha. At the same time, Marsha takes in a nephew, around the same age, when his family's house has burned down. Marsha's son vanishes. The two teenagers start having sex.

The Chicago winter is miserable for the poor, who have to walk from place to place, sitting at bus stops, waiting for buses that never seem to come. But spring comes, as always. And, in 1996, it brings, for me, a more hopeful time. It awakens with my own awakening. I study hard and party hard. I spend long, warm afternoons outside with the kids.

Everything that happens at Sue comes through Sue. Her rule can seem draconian and arbitrary. At times, she is ruled by persistent fears of injury or violence. She could ban someone from the center on a whim.

No one seems particularly bothered by this. For The Low End, as the neighborhood is called, is ruled by a similar ethos. You did not disrespect, or even disagree with, an elder. This is, in part, a legacy of the harsh rule of Jim Crow. The South is so close to the people of the south side of Chicago. It is carried in everyone, this memory of The South and its oppressiveness. Of course, Chicago in the 1990s has its own oppression to offer. Foremost is that you are told to take responsibility for yourself and that failures are yours alone to bear. We don't know that we are in this together. The teacher, the counselor, the ignorant youthworker like me, all tell these children to take responsibility, to join in the American Dream, which, by design, excludes them.

But Sue also brings an intense compassion that few could muster. She cries with people and offers them a space to cry. There is a look she can give, a look that says she cares about you, individually, that she would drop it all—the center, her good name, everything—to save this one, perfect and beautiful life. She wants to extract a person's pain. For she knows that a person lives and relives the pain of childhood for the entirety of one's life.

She scares the kids more with her theology than with her discipline. They are used to harsh discipline, and, while she is strict, she takes a radical position against beating children, and often argues with parents about it. But what scares the kids is when she tells people she doesn't believe in God. This horrifies the people. Her theology is more subtle. She points to a child of 5 or 6, and says, "Look at this child. Do you see her? Do you see how bright and beautiful she is? This is God. What more do I need?"

She has learned how to cry for herself and for the world, and knows that if she can only teach others to do so, perhaps they can save themselves.

Sue has created the center for the kids, of course. But it is also for the parents. For the community. And, not insignificantly, for her, too. It is the only place she can live, thrive, heal, survive. It's also for people like me. Like Sue, I am there because I am working to heal something buried deep within me, but I know only how to look outward. If I can only be needed enough—and the need here, among these children, is great—I can somehow overcome the wound of being told it was shameful for me to ever have needs of my own.

Sue wants me to continue at the center, but also understands that I am young and need to fly away. So we work out an unusual arrangement. I will keep working at the center, but I can take year-long sabbaticals.

It becomes apparent to me that education is one of the fundamental issues of our time. In an age of apocalypse, education cannot be about mere achievement within a collapsing system. Rather, it must be an inquiry into the collapse, a reimagining of self and world. It is telling the old stories and coming up with new ones. There's a story at once ancient and new that is present, often unspoken, on the south side of Chicago: the secret of life is to find a home when we are lost, to find kin when we are alone. This was the story of enslavement. A people who often found themselves without family, who created a culture upon the notion that family is made as much as given, verb more than noun. In this way, they became a people. And so, I find myself brought into community, for the first time feeling something more than alone. People will

often suggest to me that I ought to become a teacher, but I have no interest. For the kind of education I am seeking is right here, in the church basement.

"God grant me the serenity…" During my first winter at Sue, one of the mothers gives birth to a daughter, her fifth and last child, Serenity. I carry Serenity around in my arms, biting the skin off of apples and feeding her the meat.

4. SUE: "HOW MANY CHILDREN HAVE I BURIED?"

SUE IS IN TEARS WHEN SHE COMES TO THE DOOR. My first thought is that it must be one of the kids. She has photo albums filled with her kids, and many of them are gone. "Ronnie was such a nice kid," she might say, "and *sharp*. He was shot and killed when he was only 19."

"What happened?" I ask, referring to the tears on this particular day.

"Ken Saro-Wiwa," she says, holding up her *New York Times*. "The Nigerian poet. He's just been executed."

There are books everywhere. Stacks of papers, dogs running everywhere. There are two dogs at this particular point in Sue's life. Generally she has between one and three. There is a husky who runs circles around me. "Sit puppa," says Sue. Each of her dogs is named some version of this: "Puppa", "New Pup", etc. The husky continues her circles, ignoring Sue's pleas. Sue's hands are full. She is carrying the other dog—named "Old Dog"—along because she can no longer walk. Old Dog is also incontinent. Many have told her to put the dog to sleep. But she cannot.

I look for a place to sit down, but there is stuff everywhere. Most of it is books, papers, and toys. There is no television, no computer. It is the 1990s and Sue still has a rotary phone.

I pick up a pile of notebooks and move them from a child's chair. I sit and wait for Sue to get organized. It will take a while. She must clean the sick dog and, eventually, tie up the wild one.

I look up at her walls, her room. There is an organic wildness to it. The walls are covered with bookshelves and with pictures and newspaper clippings. There is no "art"; rather, the room, the walls, her life, is art.

"Why do we keep killing each other?" she asks.

"Well," I answer. "If you mean Saro-Wiwa, there must have been some fear on the part of the government. Totalitarian governments seem to fear poets."

Sue gently raises her gaze out the window. Her skin is wrinkled and always a little damp with some combination of sweat and tears. She always pauses before speaking.

"There are too many people," she says.

"Too many people?"

She looks off out the window and exhales deeply, meaningfully.

"Too many," she says. "Everywhere I look, people are killing people. Too many people and not enough to share."

"Is it the 'not enough' or the 'sharing' that's the problem?"

She looks at me, puzzled.

"I mean, is the problem that there are too many people or that the resources are not shared equitably?"

She exhales again. If I did not know her as I do, I'd have thought she was tiring of my difficult questions. "How many children have I buried?" she asks.

"I don't know, Sue. And I suspect you don't either."

"Many," she says.

There is a pregnant silence in the room. Our meetings are filled with these silences.

"Maybe we are asking the wrong question," she says.

"About?"

"Saro-wiwa. These children who have been murdered in Chicago. Life. Death. Even the luckiest of us only get a little bit of time. Maybe we should be grateful that Saro-wiwa did well with the time he had."

"He told his story," I say.

"He was alive," she says.

"There is little more one can ask."

We pause again. Looking out the window at her little back yard, shaking to life even on this blustery, autumn day. In a few moments, we begin to discuss the children and their lives. Matters of Life and Death.

5. CHICAGO
1996-97

Ecce deus fortiori me,
qui veniens dominabitur mihi

During the summer of 1996 I live in a sort of urban commune. I've just graduated from school and am actively unambitious. I have a job—working at Sue—that requires me to work only from midafternoon to the early evening. This gives me long summer days to read and long summer nights to smoke and drink.

I still have access to the University of Chicago library and take books out regularly, reading them throughout the day on our front porch while others, inside, head off to 9-5s or recover from hangovers. I wander the stacks, seeing what I might find. I especially like the religion section, row after row, in the darkness, of humanity's attempts to figure out who we are, where we've come from, and why. One aisle might yield the *Upanisads*; the next, the Baha'i faith.

I come upon other things. One day I find a book about the Welsh immigrants to Scranton, Pennsylvania. I know my grandfather came from there. I thumb through it to discover a photo of my great grandfather, The Reverend Teifion Richards.

I learn the sad story of the Gullah people of the Sea Islands, where we vacationed when I was a child. They lived there since the civil war in isolation, with a unique culture and language. But when developers come—such as those who built the condo we stayed in when we visited—the Gullah people are priced out. I remember the poor people living in shacks on the mainland from my childhood.

I read poets and politics, novels and religious texts. Whatever I can find. I talk about it all—revolution and music, art and the apocalypse—deep into the hot summer nights.

Quietly, secretly, I keep dreaming of the world beyond. I have yet to reach the time in my life when dreams of things past will come to me. It isn't so much a question of past and future, these dreams. It is much more inside and out. I am looking outward, to the great mystery of the world. I have to figure out how to make that great cosmos something within me. I have to fall in love with it.

By the time I return from work people have started to fill our front porch. We listen to Hip Hop and reggae, spinning Bob Marley records on an old turntable; listening to A Tribe Called Quest and Black Moon cassettes; to cool jazz samples turned from by Pete Rock's into an urban rhythm and soulful vocals transformed by Rza into the rhythm of pain, of the blend of God and sin that makes us alive.

Winston is a local rapper who freestyles on the porch. We've become great friends. He is older, and loves to regale us with stories of his childhood on the west side, where his brother was a pimp. He's a bohemian rapper with long dreadlocks, thrown into the category of "conscious MC" but really someone who just loves life more than anything. He and I discuss history and metaphysics deep into the night, every night. Robert, my college roommate, is a pre-med student, perhaps to please his father, also a doctor. He really just wants to be a musician.

He is beloved by all but struggles with loving himself. He's a collector of degrees, pieces of paper, credentials—like me, he is chasing something.

One day, we take psychedelic mushrooms, which Winston calls "The Fun Guy." First, we make it into a tea—Winston and I are the more culinary members of the group and take care of this while the others wait. We drink the disgusting mixture with glee and wait. As the effects set in, we decide to take a walk to The Point, a park on a piece of land jutting out onto Lake Michigan. We sit silently on the rocks and look along the lakefront to the buildings downtown. Clouds begin to swallow up the buildings; a cool breeze begins to blow. The waves call out to us. We look at Robert. He looks scared, staring into space.

"You OK?" asks Winston.

Robert looks at him but seems unable to speak.

"You OK?" I repeat.

Nothing.

This repeats itself for several minutes—it could be thirty seconds or an hour. I start to laugh. Winston is worried. Robert has come to a place inside, a dark place, that he does not want to face.

Then it begins to pour. We run for shelter—I laughing, Winston and Robert solemnly, silently. Robert never tells us where he went, but we all know it was a dark place, the kind of place he'll spend his whole life avoiding.

The next day is the fourth of July. We have decided to have a party and return to less soul-revealing forms of intoxication. Winston and I make a punch and harvest our homemade mango wine. We smoke a lot of weed, and Robert, who has his parents' car, takes us to the liquor store. On the way back, turn up a narrow, one-way street to look for parking.

Although it is nearly dark, Robert, as always, wears sunglasses. His seat is leaned so far back he is almost next to me as I sit in the back. Robert drives fast. "Hey, I think you missed a spot back there," says Winston. "Back at the beginning of the block."

Robert stops the car, now almost to the end of the street. He starts to back up. He is backing up fast. He picks up even more speed. My last thought is, *wow, this is the fastest I've ever backed up in a car.*

When you're moving backward in a car, it is difficult to straighten out when the wheel begins to turn. You've got to take it slow, even stop, to get it together. At 55 miles per hour, you've got no chance.

I look up. Robert is sitting next to me. He has slid into the back seat. We've crashed into a stop sign and several cars. But no one is hurt.

The party is a raging success, then a similarly raging disaster. Someone attempts to sexually assault a passed-out woman in Winston's bedroom; a whiteboy, a University kid, gets punched for talking shit to a passerby. But still, we awake with stories to talk about and ideas to share. I assume that everyone sees the infinite spreading out before them as I do, but maybe they are just trying to get by.

One day, a girl comes who catches my eye, and I hers. Brown skinned and hair just starting to lock. She shines like the sun, like the long shadows of Chicago dusk can't touch her. She's an MC and rhymes for us on the porch. The bridge of her nose wrinkles when she smiles. I don't know yet that she gets this from her mother. I don't know yet that her daughters will one day get it from her. We smoke a blunt together and try to figure it out, this girl who raps and this boy who reads poetry on the porch. We circle each other for a moment. Then she leaves. She tells me her name is Ari. I will remember it, and her, at the edges of the Earth—which is really only the edges of my self. I don't yet know the Earth is round. I have many miles to go before I'll make it back. To her.

Later that summer, I will see her at the Selassie Fest in the park, when festivals can still be free. We pass joints around and discuss the Armageddon. I assume that everyone believes, as I do. And I assume that the world isn't already ending. In those days, before everything would come to us through the Internet, music just finds you. It is like how, before we could find the perfect partner through the logarithms of a computer matchmaker, we still could fall in love.

The mystery of love is meaningless without the mystery of time. To fully love someone is to encounter not just them at that moment, but past, present, and future at once. I am not in love, yet—but that is only true if I segregate that past from the present and future. The edge between sea and sky is like this. A confluence of infinities. And this is love. There is longing, the ever-not-quiteness of it, the need we all have that can never fully be met through the encounter with the other; and there is belonging, the comfort that comes from the knowledge of being fully known. Love is fundamentally an *encounter*. An in-between things rather than a thing-itself. Love is the confluence of sky and sea, of the warmth of the Miami sun and the cold Chicago winter, the commingling of desire, the never-ending *longing* for the elusive connection to the other, and the always-present sense of *belonging* one finds in true connection. In youth, these things seem at once always present and possible, and impossibly elusive. We are so young. It is just a seed, an encounter.

Long summer days turn to dark winter nights. The party goes on. The children of Sue still come. I spend my time in basements.

I know a guy, Amon, who has been living in my dorm at the University. He is not a student; rather, he is the neighborhood dirtbag who dates a variety of women who let him move into their dorm rooms, beating them into submission and living off of them. But no one realizes all this then, and he is around. "What are you studying?" a student asks him on the elevator one day. "Oh, you know," says Amon, "a little of this and a little of that."

Amon knows this guy named Tony, a martial arts teacher. He shows up one day, asking if anyone's interested in learning. I've never thought much about martial arts, but I go along with him to meet Tony.

Tony was Special Forces in Vietnam. He brought back with him many things—and of course, left pieces of himself behind—including a variety of fighting skills he'd learned in the military. Imagine that you arrive home, to the south side of Chicago, with one skill—to kill people—and one oppositional desire—to make peace. While this may seem like an irreconcilable position, he is fortunate to have come of age during the time when many African American youth were enamored with Asian martial arts. And like many others, age and wisdom move him from the hard-styles to the internal arts. So, upon returning to the south side of Chicago from Vietnam, Tony learns the Chinese art of bagua. After many years of training, he begins to teach in his basement.

"I don't just want you to be better martial artists," he will often say. "I want you to become better *teachers*." Tony is in poor health, not in fighting shape at all. Oddly, for a man with such skill with and knowledge of the body, he eats poorly, has smoked and drank for years. While he can't kick above his waste anymore, he learns to feel and touch an opponent and, with the subtlest of movements, incapacitate him. He teaches technique with a cigarette in one hand. He often falls asleep on his couch during class. His senior students teach the younger. Down in the basement, a series of students who've trained with him for many years teach me the art.

We listen to Miles Davis while we train. "There are no wrong notes in bagua," Tony will say, paraphrasing Miles. We drink beer and smoke weed after training. "It's all a part of this, babe," Tony will say. I think he means that drinking and smoking and training with your friends are all a part of being human, and that is what he was training us to be. There is another unspoken teaching, deeper even than the art: Tony is damaged as we all are, young men with pain we didn't have words for. The art is our wordless processing, a way that we can embrace each other.

Tony came back from Vietnam to Chicago in the early 1970s. He left things there, pieces of himself. I'll never know that Tony, the one who came before Vietnam, just as I'll never know my own father, or Chicago, or the world, for that matter, before. It was around the time of my birth. He also, like everyone else who's been to Vietnam, brought things back with him. A deep and comprehensive knowledge of how to maim and kill is only one small item in his psychic suitcase.

Tony doesn't do much philosophy. It only comes out in the application. *All same same,* his teacher used to say, and he often repeats the phrase when his more literal-minded students try to get a clear answer. Everything—all technique, all battles, all of life—is a single, fluid movement.

Tony has learned to be a soldier in Vietnam, to kill or be killed—and he did much killing. But he came back to the south side of Chicago to learn how to dance. *Dancing*: That's what he calls it when we practice bagua. This is how the soldier becomes a warrior.

This was how I pass the days until it is time for me to leave. I have decided that I must go to Africa. But first, there is the Mountain.

6. THE MOUNTAIN
1997

I ARRIVE AT THE BERKSHIRES ON A BRILLIANT SUNNY DAY IN LATE AUGUST, SMOKING BIDIS AND UNCERTAIN. I've come through upstate New York, through the gloomy and depressed towns of Rochester, Syracuse, and Albany, to find myself in a new world of rural joy.

Unlike my classmates at The University of Chicago, I had no plan: no thoughts of graduate school or even of looking for a job. I sullenly graduate and continue to hang out in Hyde Park, smoking a lot of weed and working at Sue. I have no relationship to speak of. I see Ari sometimes, and we sleep together occasionally. She is wild, running all over the city with her friends, all of them beautiful and amazing women. I am most interested in running away from it all, avoiding that thing that I've been trained to fear, the thing that will kill you, I've been told: vulnerability. And I know that the best way to avoid it is to keep from falling too deeply in love. Independence, that most American of values, is what I think I have. But I don't realize yet that I am just running away from the things I really want more than anything, don't yet realize that independence is just a delusion anyway.

But I am happy and have friends, good friends. We stay up late and discuss the meaning of life, sports, and music. Many of them are artists, and I am something like that, but have no voice yet, no medium. Maybe, somewhere in Africa, I can find it.

I am largely untroubled by the question of what to do with my life. Some suggest teaching: *you like kids, ergo, you should be a teacher*. I have always liked kids, and even like teaching, but the notion of spending my days in a school seems like a slow and painful way to die. My mother, the teacher, suggests—as if she'd never met me before—I apply to law school. Perhaps this was just what comes to mind because my father is a lawyer. "But I don't want to be a lawyer, mom," I say. "I mean, like, I have zero, less than zero, interest in that." "But you could still go to law school," she retorts, undeterred. "There are lots of things you could do with a law degree." I am unconvinced, so I do nothing.

More than ambitions for a career, I have a vague desire for adventure, to see the world, and pretensions of doing good in the world. It really all comes down to this: There is something wild still left in me, and I want to go find it. I research programs in Africa to work for an NGO, without really knowing why. Mostly, I suppose, because Africa seems about as far from anything as I can imagine. And I have an intuition that the world I've been given, the stories I've been told, are unraveling.

I am looking for new stories. But first, there are the Berkshires, the site of the rural compound that serves as the training ground for "solidarity workers," volunteers who provide much of the staffing for the NGO's projects in Africa and Latin America. I find myself no longer on the flat, urban grid of the south side of Chicago, but on the side of a mountain.

As part of the Zimbabwe team, I am to spend several months there, preparing for the work I will ultimately do in Africa.

This involves a variety of things to read and some group activities. We learn buzzwords like sustainable development, learn to name-drop people like Paolo Freire. But the real work, it soon becomes apparent, is fundraising. Each person is supposed to raise a certain amount of money to finance the trip and the project. This is to be done by traveling throughout the country, standing on corners like well-dressed beggars or knocking on doors like liberal Jehovah's Witnesses.

We are young and believe in what we are doing, this generation of kids too young to be a part of a movement and too old to be attached to the world through devices of disconnected connection. But we lose faith quickly. We are the generation who has never been told what to do, the least supervised in history. Now we find ourselves part of a group. We are supposed to ask strangers for money. We all hate it and most of us are bad at it.

After hours of canvassing on a cold October day, a girl, maybe twelve years old, answers the door and runs off. "Mom! He's here!" exclaims an adolescent voice. "Get the money!" *This is it*, I think. *I have finally gotten lucky. I have finally arrived at the perfect house.* But when the mother does arrive, she looks at me with an expression of exaggerated disappointment. "You're not the pizza man, are you?" she says. They give me nothing.

People are shockingly stingy and generous, rude and welcoming. Most who give know little and care even less about Africa, but give in the name of our youthful enthusiasm, the one thing we have. As much as I hate it, I am grateful to learn to see America from a new vantage point. We drive down in a dilapidated van to New York and D.C., drive across the country as far west as Milwaukee. We scrounge leftover food from restaurants and sleep in church basements, like atheist evangelists. And this is what we are: Europe has shed, perhaps, something of its Christianity, but remains as paternalistic as ever.

Back on the side of the mountain, summer turns into autumn. With no weed to smoke, I take up rolling my own cigarettes, which I do each evening with great pleasure, looking over the side of the mountain to the east. I walk through mountain trails and learn to be entombed in the changing colors, remembering the joy of warm autumn days of my childhood. It's not the view from the side of the road, where the tourists take their pictures, but *inside* the forest, in their womb of color. There, you can see and smell and feel the forest turning to compost, preparing to be reborn.

Autumn turns to winter. We are virtually trapped on the compound and with each fundraising trip the pressure grows.

I chop my own Christmas tree and set it up in the common area. The Danish leaders are unsure what to do with such a pious, American gesture.

The nighttime sky explodes in color each night, stars so close they almost seem reachable. I've never seen a sky like this, never knew how many stars were really out there.

Finally, we meet the fundraising goal. We have our tickets for Africa. We meet up in New York City a few days before the New Year, 1997. I meet up with college friends: I smoke blunts laced with coke on New Year's Eve with my college friend Luis from the Bronx; I spend a day and a night with my old roommate, Hung, a Vietnamese refugee who has become an investment banker, and realize that already we have nothing to talk about. The earth is spinning fast. We take off on a direct flight to Johannesburg, flying deep into the night. We could be flying anywhere, to Peoria or to Stockholm. But we are flying to Africa.

7. ZIMBABWE
1998

During the second to last week I work in Zimbabwe the price of bread triples overnight. *There are strikes and riots in the cities. Mugabe is condemned by the West. The West is condemned by Mugabe. In the bush, the earth cracks in the dry air as the sun continues to beam down, day after rainless day.*

The Baobab trees are unmoved.

We arrive in Johannesburg disoriented: First, we've been on a plane for 18 hours, in that sterile and nonlocal space. Second, we have left New York City and, in the blink of an eye, find ourselves in Africa. And at the same time, there is a remarkable similarity. The wealth of Jo'burg is stunning. Glittering malls and shiny Mercedes. Somewhere, we know, there is also poverty beyond which most of us have seen. But we don't see it. Exhausted, we wander through a mall—such a disappointment for youthful Westerners primed for wild Africa. We sleep—or rather, in our jet-lagged state, pretend to sleep—in a Rasta youth hostel before heading to Zimbabwe in the morning.

The day we arrive in Zimbabwe, the currency collapses. There are riots in the streets of Harare over the price of bread. Mugabe blames the West; the West blames Mugabe. The streets of Harare teem with frustrated masses, while on the countryside, the peasants work as they always have, day after day.

I have been assigned to work on a project in the Eastern Highlands, in a region known as Manicaland. Because of my teaching experience, I am given the role of a teacher in the adult literacy project. There are two projects, and this one is farther from Harare, and more remote in general, than the other. So those heading to the north of Harare are shuttled away, while the four of us heading to the east are sent to a hostel and told to wait for Bennie, the project manager, who will pick us up and take us to the east.

This is Africa. An African city that buzzes with the electricity of all the paradoxical joy and anger that Africa is. It has a rhythm, a vibrancy. And at the same time, Harare is a place of extraordinary poverty. This is the new Africa, the Africa that has been growing since the quasi-independence of the neo-colonial age: as rural life is undermined through global economic forces and, increasingly, climate change, the rural people move to the cities, and usually to the one megacity that is surrounded by shantytowns to house them. I know these rhythms, and this despair, from the south side of Chicago. But there is something different here, something more extreme than anything I've seen.

I spend these days in a daze, wandering the streets and fighting off beggars. Men sell Shona sculptures that would go for hundreds of dollars in the U.S. for mere pennies; children beg in packs. Just as the plane ride has transported me from the dead of the New York winter to the tropics, it has also converted me from beggar to the begged. And just as I struggled with asking people for money, I now struggle with the question of giving or not giving it away. I have become immeasurably wealthy. My US dollars—even though I don't have that many—buy me things far beyond the means of most Zimbabweans. I can eat, for a few bucks, at the best restaurants in Harare. But more than that, there are the encounters on the street. Dozens of children hound me for food and for money. I learn quickly that to give away anything to one means the others will come after me even harder. I learn to avoid eye contact, and feel profoundly what this does to me. Why shouldn't I just give away all that I have? And then there are the hawkers—usually young men, standing on a corner, selling something, anything, from advice to works of art. They are easier to dismiss—an annoying thirty-year-old brings less guilt than a child. But, of course, I know that they have children to feed, too. I am learning, now, the life of the Westerner in the "third world."

After a few days, Bennie comes to pick us up. A taciturn Dane, Bennie seems never to smile. So expressionless is his face, I can't tell if he speaks of his work with self-deprecation or simple disdain for the people he's worked with. There is little romance in his Africa. Or his image of Africans. But I, like the others, am ready to listen to him. He has lived in Africa, after all. He is more worldly and experienced than any of us. We are idealistic little shits; he doesn't need sentimentality when it comes to Zimbabwe. He knows its harsh reality and has devoted his life to its development. This is what we think, and need to believe, as we listen to him talk to us, driving in his pickup out of teeming Harare and into the bush, watching the packs of men swing their scythes to cut the grass alongside the highway, watching the children wave to us as we zoom past them.

We stop briefly in Mutare, Zimbabwe's third largest town and the main city in the region. It is small, manageable, and mellow—nothing like Harare. Then we proceed northward toward the Nganga national park, into the foothills. The weather there is milder than the rest of Zimbabwe, which, at this time of year, is stiflingly hot and humid. Most of this land is "communal", which means it is the place where the indigenous people are to farm for their survival, as opposed to the commercial farms which are run by the white Rhodesians—and, increasingly, by Mugabe's cronies. This is savannah, rolling and rocky grassland dotted with the occasional mopane or baobab tree. Young men and boys tend cows and goats, while women walk in lines with enormous containers of water on their heads. It is breathtakingly beautiful. The mornings are mistfilled, creating an aura of mystery to the place.

Our farm is located on the top of a hill. An old farm, destroyed in the war for independence, the NGO has taken it over and is slowly rebuilding it. Empty shells of buildings still dot the landscape. My own room overlooks one such shell, as well as a vast valley. Each morning, I rise to the mistfilled mountains; each evening, I contemplate the setting sun, the periwinkle and ever-so-brief tropical dusk, and, finally, the splendor of the southern nighttime skies, Orion doing cartwheels across the firmament.

Bennie imposes a Danish efficiency on the project. I am working in the adult literacy program. Each day we are to meet with a group in a particular village at a specific time at a designated meeting place. The meeting place is sometimes outside, under a tree perhaps, but often we meet in the kitchen, where the women are cooking. They'll feed us and talk rapidly in Shona to my teaching partner, Maxwell, laughing at my attempts at speaking Shona.

I've read Freire and think I've come to teach literacy as liberation, but the Danes are teaching something else—the gospel of development. In order to enter into the global capitalist order, people have to learn to abstract their time. So, meetings are set at a time. 1:00, perhaps. But in Manicaland, in the bush, they know, like Einstein knew, that time and events cannot be separated. They know what 1:00 is: it is after the water has been fetched, the crops tended, the children fed. When those activities are completed, never before, regardless of what a watch might say, class can begin. We often wait for hours, eating and talking in the African sun. We think they are always late; but we are always early.

"Good morning, teddeeeeee!"

Each morning I pass by the little school on the farm. The children call to me from the swings.

"*Mangwanani!*" I answer in Shona. They laugh uproariously as they swing higher, higher. There is nothing funnier in Zimbabwe than a *murungu* speaking Shona.

Mwana Ndi Amai is scrawled on one side of the school: "The Child is the Mother."

Umuntu ngumuntu ngabantu says the other side: "*A person is a person through persons.*"

The workers can be heard in the distance, singing their work songs—the men deep and melancholy, the women at once hopeful and sad.

There is an unfathomable isolation I feel in this place at the edge of Zimbabwe. I can look out each day across the mountains, to Mozambique, which seems to me to be the farthest place in the world, and each night, into the black and empty sky, where I see star formations come together the likes of which I've never seen in my urban existence. My favorite time is dusk—so short in the tropics that one has to be careful not to miss it—when the long work of the hot day has been finished and the air begins to cool, when the darkening sky still reveals enough of the landscape for journeys overland to be imagined, but also just dark enough to reveal the earliest and brightest stars. This is the edge between dark and light, the edge where, in spite of its tropical brevity, I feel I always reside these days.

Power outages are commonplace, although no one in our region besides the wealthy and larger institutions, like ours, has power. Rare, however, are airplanes. Only a few times while I am in Africa do I see one. Each time I remark at how odd it is to see them so infrequently. Perhaps, however, what I can't yet see is how strange it truly is to live in a time and place when airplanes overhead *are* commonplace, this blip in the geo-historical process when we burn away our fossil fuels as fast as we can, racing around the planet, thinking we are going somewhere, as if it isn't round. I can't yet see these things, but I do begin to notice the wonder of an airplane—a sensation I will never lose—and imagine where they might be going.

News of the events in Zimbabwe and beyond reaches us slowly. The streets of Harare burn from time to time. Mugabe is feeling the pressure, and the purges that marked the early days of independence return. He also begins to remove white farmers from their land. There is much criticism. These are the *"good"* white farmers, after all, the ones who stayed after independence to build a new Zimbabwe. White liberals cringe and wring their hands, unable to reconcile the obvious injustice that remains in Zimbabwe and their personal dislike of Mugabe and sympathy with the white farmers. I have little sympathy for the white farmer in Zimbabwe.

News from abroad comes even slower. What I can't see is that the streets of Harare are no different from the streets in the West, the growing protest movements that begin to awake. My sleepy generation, unsupervised enough to party ourselves into oblivion; post-civil-rights, we've been told that that collective struggle was over: *"get yours"* is the new battle cry. Without a Vietnam to scare our privileged sons, we simply try to grab more and more of the world that, we were told, is ours. Or perhaps, we are grabbing for more and more of a world that is falling apart: we are, all of us, the colonials, packing up our good china on the way to the airport, one last time. This experiment—bigger even than colonialism—is crashing down. Perhaps I'm not so different from the Rhodesians.

At the same time, things are coming together that I cannot yet see. South Central LA burns first, then the shantytowns of Harare. Later, while I watch the stars of the south sky from the eastern highlands, protests flare up in Seattle and Turin.

Other news comes, too, brought to us on the bus from Mutare. Mail here is left at the local store, for there is no post office. There are letters and pictures from the Children's Center. I put them all over the wall next to my bed. Maxwell, my partner, comes by and looks at them, thoughtfully. I can tell he has questions. "Teddy," he asks, "these pictures you have, all the people in them are *Black*." I explain to him about Chicago, America, slavery, and Black people in my country.

Another letter comes from a brilliant student at the Children's Center who will one day have Ivy League diplomas all over her wall, who will one day, like me, work for NGOs in Africa, looking for things she can't find at home. She tells me that her brother has been murdered, tears staining the page, ink running and blurred—it is as if I can see the world as she now did, through her tears. But of course, I can't.

The earlier part of my job in Zimbabwe is centered on creating lesson plans and recruiting participants. There is a team of five of us. Wilson, the leader, organizes the rest into two groups of two. I am partnered with Maxwell. Tall and impossibly skinny, Maxwell seems to float across the rolling savannah as we walk from village to village, meeting with women who will invariably feed us and promise to come to our classes. We pick the low hanging mangos as we sit under trees to share our lunch. Maxwell offers me a series of queries, always about America, which, for him, is a great and vexing puzzle.

"In America," he begins, "are there rural areas, like this?" He bites into the mango, exposing its sweet and juicy flesh, and quickly spits out the skin. His movements, like his speech, are always sharp and crisp, but gentle. It is a blisteringly hot day, and we have walked many miles, down into the ruggedly steep, humid and malarial Honde Valley. We've stopped to rest, and to await the matriarchs of the village to schedule a class. It is the rainy season, but the rains have been sparse. The humidity is still brutal.

"Yes," I answer. "There are many. But they are different."

"More developed?"

"Yes."

Maxwell ponders this for a moment as he hands me another bun he's purchased from the rural shop we passed on the way—it is unthinkable to buy oneself food or eat without sharing in Zimbabwe.

"In America, where you are from…"

Maxwell is the eldest son in his family. His parents have died, leaving him to care for his younger siblings alone. This means managing his menial, subsistence farm; working all day, every day for the NGO; and sending the younger ones to school. He works as a teacher because he is smart—that is obvious—but he could have and should have gone further in school than he has, could have and should have had a position of more authority than he has. What becomes obvious to me, fairly quickly, is that the old colonial pattern of promoting mediocrity and accommodation remains in Zimbabwe.

"In America, what are the Black people's lives like?"

Those who ask questions remain stuck, behind those who are less threatening to those in power.

It is nearly impossible to understand what it might mean to be born, as Maxwell was, in colonial Africa. An occupied nation, an apartheid state. But like most little boys, politics would not have been his concern. He would have hoped for less hunger, perhaps, or more opportunities, but his days were spent playing and working and going to school. There was lack, of course, but there was also beauty. He walked the paths of his ancestors. He knew who he was.

My job is absurd, really. I am to be "teaching" these people, women who have lived through wars, who have raised children on whatever they can grow in these cramped and parched lands. I am a kid. These are women.

I mostly follow Maxwell. In the communal lands surrounding the district center of Mutasa, death is everywhere. There is little access to health care and the land is unyielding and stretched far beyond its limits.

Often, people come knocking on my door for an ibuprofen—any form of medication is rare. And to find one's way to any kind of health care facility can be an arduous journey. Early in my time in Zimbabwe, I contract malaria, probably on one of my journeys into the hot and mosquito-infested

Honde Valley. What starts as some mild nausea becomes an unrelenting combination of vomiting and diarrhea. A friend tries to take me to the doctor, but I can't even make it to the road where we would catch the bus. This is probably for the best. The bus ride would be miserable.

I juggle vomiting and diarrhea—no easy task—while pausing, ever so briefly as I stagger to the toilet, to marvel at the beauty of the country.

AIDS, in addition to malaria, ravishes the countryside. A coworker dies and everyone from the project attends the funeral. For hours we walk and pray and weep and sing. The men dig the grave in the dry red earth with shovels and pickaxes and hands. The women ululate, then weep, then sing. *"Jesu,"* they sing, *"Jesu Chete."* Only Jesus.

It is this world into which Maxwell was born. And it is in this world that his parents died young, leaving Maxwell to care for his family, and their land. We walk for miles together every day, as he tells me about his life, about his family, and I tell him about America, a subject which never ceases to fascinate him. We ride buses, the conductors hanging off the side to wrangle the passengers at full speed, then leaping back on the as the buses speed off; we squeeze on to combis, minivans that pack us in like sardines; and we occasionally hitchhike—we pay for these rides, too, and they are sometimes precarious. Once, a drunk driver almost causes me to fly off the back of a pick up.

We don't teach much, especially me, but we learn—especially me. Occasionally we find enough women to teach. They come with babies on their backs, water on their heads, and other loads, unseen but heavier. These are women who've lived through so much as powerful men have made, and continue to make, decisions that have transformed their lives and land, the place their ancestors were sent by the British so the colonizers could take the good land for commercial farms. Some women, most of them, are too old to even know their age. Those women come simply because it is something they can do to be free. We give them a pencil and begin to teach them to write their name.

One woman comes to every class who is so old she doesn't know her age or birth date, so old she's raised children and grandchildren and great grandchildren on what she could grow in the parched earth, the land that the British gave her grandmothers when they'd stolen the fertile land. She's never held a pencil. I don't recall her name, but I know it begins with a C, because that is as far as she ever gets: every day, she sits on the ground, practicing her crooked Cs, wrinkled like her skin, while I contemplate the absurdity of having flown halfway around the planet, a 25 year old with liberal arts degree, to teach this woman, who must have more wisdom in her crooked Cs than in my alphabet of credentials.

The workers on the farm have formed a football team, and I become a member. Most of the teaching crew, including Maxwell, are less athletic types. The farm laborers make up the core of the team. I've played a bit—throughout high school—and am a good athlete, strong and fit, but understand the game very little, having really cut my teeth in the city, playing basketball. Most play barefoot on the hard and sparsely grass-covered pitch. My feet, of course, can't handle this at all. I wear my expensive American sneakers.

The Africans play with freedom and joy. And they are not only fit and athletic, but also incredibly gifted technically. Bennie is a good player, too. A bit older and slower than the younger players, but skilled enough to be effective and possessing a European tactical awareness the rest of us lack. His attitude on the pitch is as dour as off it. He complains of the tendency of the Africans to try dribbles and tricks when passing and discipline would be more effective. What he cannot see—and what I can because of my days in the parks in urban America—is that the game is only secondarily about winning: its true purpose is to find freedom and space, to find a way to express oneself. This is important for a people who cannot even farm the best land in their own country. Benny could never understand this.

Chigara lives in a nearby house and is the vet, caring for the cows and providing a paternal presence on the farm. He is also the football coach. As no one on the team speaks English, all the instructions are given in Shona. I know enough to know that I've gotten very little good coaching in my life and that Chigara knows far more than I about the game.

I can never understand the tactics—they are explained largely in Shona and based on specific systems that everyone but me seems to understand. But I am fast enough and strong enough to get by. Our first match is against Mutasa D.C., the nearby administrative center. The crowd taunts me mercilessly—a white man playing soccer is, evidently, as funny as one who tries to speak Shona. I've been in these situations before and wasn't especially bothered, but I played poorly anyway, missing a sitter.

I don't score until the final match I play in Zimbabwe, a match that, not long after my goal, descends into a brawl that I watch dumbly and without really comprehending why. I've scored my goal and am happy.

As the rains slow, word of Zimbabwe's disintegration spreads even into the countryside. Stories of unrest and repression in the cities arrives as if from another country. In the eastern highlands, and at the NGO, we concern ourselves primarily with the politics of the local. Bennie rules the project as his own fiefdom, and puts those Africans in positions of power who are most amenable to his rule and decisions. Among the white people and even among his most trusted—and uneducated, for Chigara would never be privy to such confidences—lieutenants, he disparages anything African. "You wouldn't believe this shit these bush people believe," he'll say. He warns us over both their primitive beliefs as well as their untrustworthiness. He forbids women to travel alone, for fear of their being raped.

Benny is a member of what was called "The Teachers Group". These are the insiders, a group of people committed to the cause of development work throughout the third world. They have agreed not only to do the work, but also to pool their resources. "Common economy, common time, common distribution," reads the tagline. Nothing wrong with this, to my mind, or to any of the other solidarity workers.

They started out as hippies, driving school buses to Kathmandu from Denmark, and later from North America to Central America. And like us, many of them turned away from the self-indulgence of the hippy movement to try to make the world a better place. So they built schools and farms. Development work, it is called.

Others call it a cult. We begin to hear rumors: The Teachers Group owns vast plantations in Latin America. The Teachers Group is stealing money meant for development work. And, at the same time, the people I meet there, the African members of The Teachers Group, are not getting rich. Quite the opposite: they own nothing. And they seem to believe deeply in the work they do.

More than once, our house is robbed at night while we sleep. They steal pots and pans, blankets, anything they can carry. The local police always find someone to blame and take them to the police station to beat a confession out of them. Our position as aid workers is complex—we are wealthy beyond the imagination of the local people, privileged in unfathomable ways. We think we are helping in some way, but also know deep down we are not. The colonial system is powerful, and its cruel genius is laid bare in the way that Africans with just a little bit of power use it against other Africans.

Problems arise for the aid workers when a group of us begin to go into Mutare to experience the nightlife. Bennie disapproves. When he gets wind of it, he tells all the foreign staff—mostly Europeans and Americans—not to go into town alone and never to go out to hear music. "These are bushmen," he tells us. "You don't know what you are getting into."

We go anyway, and hear Oliver Mtukudzi play in a drab and secluded bar in Mutare. His music, bringing together the patterns of traditional mbira music and the instrumentation of the West, is joyful. "Hear me Lord," he sings out in English, sounding something like the lamentations of Christian churches I've known, and then continuing on in Shona, crying out in words I can't understand to gods I don't know. His voice is deep, sorrowful, hopeful. An intimation of the possibility of joy in a world of suffering—the possibility that you can still dance when your world is falling apart.

We continue to hear more and more condescending comments about the "natives." The two Danish solidarity workers admire Bennie greatly and parrot his comments.

Among the Zimbabweans, there emerge two classes: the workers and those slotted to become a part of the Teachers Group. My teammates on the football team are all workers, but they speak almost no English and my Shona isn't good enough to ask them much. Besides, they wouldn't know even as much as I do about DAPP.

The Teachers Group, on the other hand, has been told not to say much about their role, but I am able to discern two things. First, I learn that they earn no money; their "salaries" are pooled and used for the NGO's projects. Second, no one who would question this system would ever be asked to join the Teachers Group.

Because Maxwell is my partner and, in my opinion, the smartest and most effective teacher we have, I ask him.

We sit under a tree one day, waiting for class to start. If it will.

"Why haven't you been asked to be in the Teacher's Group? I mean, even Bennie knows that you are the best person we got in organizing and teaching these lessons." It's true. Bennie knows that there are few people who can organize people, whom people trust, as Maxwell. He is sober and easy to talk to and is a father figure to his younger siblings.

Maxwell only smiles. "I only have my ZABEC 5," he answers, referring to the level of school he's completed. "I had to leave school when my parents died."

"Development" seems like a good idea. But the funny thing is this: everyone associated with development seems to be suffering. For it requires entrance into the neocolonial order. It turns men into workers and renders the traditional work of women—raising children, non-commercial agriculture—meaningless. A man's value comes to be associated with his paycheck, which never measures up to those he encounters in the market economy. Men are forced to move around the country, the continent, the planet, in search of bigger paychecks. Families fall apart. They bring home a little money. And AIDS. They bring home despair at their loss of place in the world. And the women suffer the worst. I see this every day, as we roam the countryside, teaching women to read and write, as if a third-grade education could make up for their absent or dead husbands, a new world order that values nothing they've done or can offer. Lives and land are recrafted to fit the global economy—that is what development means. And I find myself a part of that process.

The rainy season passes, and the misty mornings turn to clear, mild, and dry days. There is never a cloud in the sky. And the nights are now clear and cool. I've never seen so many stars. Each night I sit out on the bench in front of my room, watching the Zodiac encircling the firmament. Our days are spent walking, always walking. Occasionally, we teach classes, but mostly we walk and talk and wait.

I've been watching Mozambique across the valley and have dreamt of going there. It seems as far as a person could get. I am determined to get a visa on my trip to Harare.

I have some time to explore the country first and go with some friends to the south to Chimanimani Park. I camp in a guava grove with two guys named Jason. We spend the next few days marveling at the rock formations and get terribly lost. My plan to follow a river back home backfires when we run up against a huge cliff that drops off for what looks like miles. But we eventually find a firebreak and make our way back before nightfall.

We keep on to the south, to the dusty lands surrounding the ruins of Great Zimbabwe. This part of the country is even more remote and feels poorer than the eastern highlands. We crisscross the country, hitchhiking on the backs of lorries and in cars driven by bitter old Rhodesians who will tell you, if you care to sit up front and chain-smoke for a while, how they've built this country themselves and Mugabe was ruining it. There are no innocents between the Rhodesians and Mugabe. They've both left a country in ruins far less romantic than Great Zimbabwe. This is Modern Zimbabwe, a failing nation-state.

Roger, one of these men, gives us a ride somewhere between Hwange National Park and Victoria Falls. I've found myself sharing cigarettes in the cab while the Jasons sleep in the back of the pickup. He is just beginning to explain the tangled story of his own Africanness, Mugabe, and the post-colonial economy when he pauses, looking out the window and sniffing. "A veld fire!" he exclaims.

I've barely processed what he's said when I see it—flames rising up in a line across the savannah. We watch carefully as it burns. I can't tell him much about this country that he believes is his, even if he can see only a vision warped with whiteness. We talk no more.

From Victoria Falls we rent a truck and ride out to the village of Binga on the banks of the Zambezi, known among outsiders for its marijuana cultivation and drummaking. We sleep in a house on stilts, warned not to leave at night because the hippos come to graze. We listen, both to the advice and to the grunting hippos beneath.

From there, I send Ari a postcard. She will save it, and it will sit on my desk, as it has for some time, with the idea that we ought to frame it. She is surprised to receive it, she says, surprised that I am thinking about her. I sent lots of postcards in those days, I will say, a partial truth that masks a bigger lie, like the lies I told about why I left.

I return to Harare where I've traveled regularly now for months. It is a different world, and I see it differently than when I first arrived. There is the poverty and crime, of course, but it is also a bustling, cosmopolitan place, a cultural center not only in Zimbabwe, but also in all of southern Africa. There is art and music and restaurants. The shops have more than Coke and sadza.

I get my visa in Harare—secretly, for the NGO forbids us to travel out of our assigned country—but when I arrive at the dusty border with Mozambique a few weeks later, I am told that the dates are wrong. I argue with the disinterested man behind the counter while the man next to me chuckles and mutters about me in Portuguese: *"Preocupado? Preocupado?"*

"Well," he tells me, "if you have American dollars you can pay for an expedited visa right now."

"How much?" I ask, vaguely aware that this is a bribe, not an "expedited visa".

"How much do you have?" he asks.

I pull out a twenty—I have perhaps $80 US on me—and he is satisfied. I go on, and walk down the muddy road into the poorest country on earth, only a few years removed from a war that has been largely funded by my own country that has left it with almost no infrastructure. One could be forgiven for being skeptical of aid workers like me. I don't care: don't care about the bribe, about my own Americanness or privilege. I am free and ready to fly.

8. MOZAMBIQUE
1998

It is likely that most of the mountain people of the borderland area between Zimbabwe and Mozambique have never seen the sea. The thing is, it really isn't that far. That's the privilege I have: I can cross borders, travel distances that may have taken generations for my ancestors. Or at least would only have been traversed in one direction—a migrant is a very different thing from a tourist. I'm not exactly a tourist. I've been an aid worker; I've been living in the "bush". Now I am headed to the beach.

"What is your *question*?" says the man on the back of the flatbed truck as he gives me a guava. It is an odd turn of phrase; perhaps his English is not so good and he means something else. After all, even on the other side of the border, the English-speaking side, most do not speak much English. Here, on the Mozambican side, I figure most speak Portuguese, perhaps Shona and some other African languages, but not English.

"What do you mean?" I ask, squinting into the wind and sun as we race down from the mountains into the flatlands.

His English is good. "You are coming a long way," he says, passing me another guava. I feel like he doesn't merely refer to the distance from the border to the sea. "You do not look like a business man or a refugee. You must be trying to answer some question."

I bite into the guava and toss the skin off the truck and onto the high grass that borders the sorry road. I taste its sensuous dance of sweet and sour, the texture of its crunchy seeds and soft flesh. There are other tastes and textures, too, and I taste them: wind blowing through my long hair, the smell of burning garbage, the joy of the road. I am *alive*. The answer to his question is there—or, rather, the question—but I cannot articulate it. We smile at each other, sharing the fruit of the poorest country in the world, racing through the bush, to the sea, saying nothing.

I arrive in Beira to expectant smiles. This is the poorest country on Earth, not very far removed from a disastrous civil war that stretched out beyond years and into generations. I am grabbed quickly by a smiling cabby. "Where do you go?"

"Bique's."

"Ah yes," he says, smiling broadly. "I know this place. This is a good place."

He shoves me into the backseat of a dilapidated old car and says something incomprehensible to the driver. Apparently, in Mozambique, driving a taxi is a two-person job. Before he even gets in the car, his partner starts the engine. It sputters weakly. He shouts something again and begins to push, the door still open. Again, the engine sputters. Finally, it starts, and before it takes off, the man leaps into the front seat of the slowly accelerating car. None of this particularly surprises me; I've watched, for many months, the acrobatics of bus conductors as they sing their destination and jump in and out of their moving buses. We are off.

We leave the area of the Beira bus station and head north, through the kind of scenery one might expect near the sea: tall grass waving in the salty breeze, palm trees. For a moment, I wonder if the men will actually take me to my destination, if this won't be some sort of robbery attempt. I've been robbed a couple of times before. But it is a brief moment of uncertainty. I am young. And, you see, the risk is worth it. I am answering my question, that unarticulated and unknown question that I can, at that moment, only answer in Beira, Mozambique.

Finally, we reach the place. I thank the men and give them a wad of Metacais—worth only pennies but enough that they seem satisfied. I enter an incredibly modern-looking bar, equipped with satellite television and a view of the beach. For a few dollars I can pitch my tent on the beach next to the bar; I can use their bathrooms and drink their liquor and cappuccino. White sands stretch out across a vast and empty and clean beach dotted with fishermen and boys playing soccer. An occasional shipwreck. The ocean shines in a bright blue against a slightly lighter and cloudless sky. The World Cup plays on the satellite television: Zidane is working his magic for a French team filled with Africans. Here, in the poorest country in the world, I have found paradise.

As the days pass, a few friends, fellow aid workers, join me in Beira. This is a different time: we've communicated through letters, vague addresses scratched on pieces of paper. But they've found me.

We spend our days on the beach and wandering through the old town. The streets, twisted and nameless, are at once splendorous in their colonial architecture and desperate in their poverty. We enter an old theater that has been converted into a restaurant; on market days we buy cashews from old Indian women as the men sip coffee in the square; squatters have moved into a luxurious old hotel and grow fruit trees on the roof.

I jog along the beach each morning, passing by the occasional shipwreck along with boys playing football—future Zidanes or, perhaps, Eusebios—and the fishermen pushing their boats out to sea. The port, too, is filled with shipwrecks, "Welcome to Atlantic City" scrawled on the side of one.

I return to the sea and watch, eating coconuts and swimming in the ocean. The waves offer themselves to me—even in the darkness of night, I listen to them. Each wave is different, unique; each returns to the same sea. This, I can see, can hear, can feel, is the rhythm of life.

In the evenings a few locals come to the beach bar to watch the world cup, but mostly there are other travelers—white Zimbabweans and South Africans, plus a few aid workers like me. After living in the bush for so long, I enjoy watching Zidane and drinking espresso.

There is an inkling of something happening that we've only begun to understand. Globalization and Global Warming are words we've heard a lot of in the 1990s, but I don't really understand what they mean yet, don't understand the perilous and shrinking world in which we all live.

There is also something awakening in me. I've gotten a taste of the backpacker scene as a college student in Spain and in the hostels in Harare. I want to go. I want to go and not stop. To feel the sensation of the wind in my hair as in that flatbed. I am in Mozambique, at the edge of the world. Whatever my question was, I can only ask it here.

The problem is that, in a shrinking world, there are so few edges. Only centers. No questions. Only answers.

As the days pass, my aid-worker friends leave. I am there alone again—eating coconuts and watching the sea. On my last night there, I emerge from the bar to find that it is raining. It has been the dry season; and it has been so long since I've seen even a rain cloud that I haven't even considered the possibility. My ragged little tent, which I've borrowed from a friend and had no rain flap, is filling with water.

The bar is now closed, so I try to sleep in the wet tent. Rain drips through the top of the tent, onto my things, onto my head, into my hands—rain, that will return to the sea and be no different than the pulsating waves, the wetness of my own tears. I quickly give up and retreat with whatever dry possessions I can gather into the only dry place I can find—the bathroom.

As bathrooms go—particularly bathrooms in impoverished, war-ravaged countries—this one is actually remarkably clean and bright. But it is no place to sleep, and I quickly abandon the idea.

I take out my journal and began to write. This is nothing new. I've been writing every day for months about my travels, my encounters, my thoughts and feelings about the new world I am encountering both beyond me and within my own heart. But on that night, I do something different. I begin to write a story.

I am born in Mozambique. I enter the ocean and emerge as a man, a storyteller. I watch the rains pour down into my tent, raindrops dropping into my hands like the blood of my child, many years later. Bloody and quivering, like me, like the entire world. Alive.

I come back into Zimbabwe on the back of a pickup driven by a bunch of South Africans. I am wet and tired and munch sporadically on a coconut until, as we stop back at the border, a monkey leaps from a tree and takes it from me.

The South Africans are kind to me and take me all the way to the youth hostel in Harare where I am to await my flight back to New York.

I fly off to New York City, its air-conditioning, its stores and its restaurants, and Zimbabwe falls apart. The currency crashes again and again. The stores are empty. Mugabe bulldozes neighborhoods, tortures his opponents, ruins the economy. Armed gangs take over white farms. The people are hungry. Everyone who can, leaves. But they won't leave like I do, won't go to places where they can sip lattes and buy new clothes. They leave for South Africa and Europe and America, where they are scorned and called cockroaches and illegals and worse, where they clean toilets and die of AIDS, leaving behind starving mothers and wives and children.

Zimbabwe falls apart, and I leave because I can—I leave the rolling hills of Manicaland, leave the warm sadza in my hands, leave the parched red soil, the lowing cows, the work songs. I leave behind the texture of the Earth, Africa, and ride on an air-conditioned airplane, over the Atlantic, over the cries of the ancestors of my unborn, unimagined children. I sleep fitfully, awakening often, not remembering where I am, where I've come from, or where I'm going, unsure if it even matters in the sterile air of the airplane, looking down at the earth reduced to two-dimensions, without depth. I dream that I am Icarus, falling into the sea. This is where my story begins.

Something has emerged on the other side of that dark night spent in a bathroom in the poorest country on Earth. Tired and wet as I am, I feel no despair. As the storm seems to come out of the sea, something emerges from the ocean of my own heart, swollen and bloody and gasping for air. There was someone new born on the other side.

But I have many miles to go. I still don't even know what my question is, much less have an answer for it. I know only that I have reached that particular moment through a confluence of stories. And I have to listen to them clearly. I have to find them; I know that there is a story in which I am participating, one that I have to go out into the world to embrace and uncover to even comprehend who I might be; and I know that there is a story I need to tell.

Many years later I will learn that when something is being born, it is my job to catch it.

PART II
PURGATORIO

Io ritornai dalla santissim'onda
Rifatto si, come piante novelle
Rinnovellate di novella fronda,
Puro e disposto a salire alle stelle.

—Dante, Purgatorio, Canto XXXIII, 142-145

9. NORTH AMERICA
1998-99

I RETURN FROM AFRICA IN THE SUMMER OF 1998 KNOWING THAT I HAVE THINGS TO DO, A WORLD TO WHICH I WANT TO RETURN. *I have been to the wilderness, found my own wildness, but want to come back after my forty days and forty nights.*

But the truth is that I really don't want to return. I want to wander. What's more, I want to run away. I have learned that the thing I want is also the thing I fear most: intimacy. And so, I learn to perpetually look for connection even as I run from it, a running from and a running to: I am afraid to confront my own demons, and the perpetual motion of the journey away allows me to avoid intimacy with self. At the same time, I am trying to fall in love, but only have the courage to fall in love with an abstraction: the world as a whole, its brokenness and its beauty. There's something necessary, I will later come to see, about this wandering. I need to experience the world like this in order to know what's so broken in myself.

We fly from South Africa back to New York. Eighteen hours on a cramped plane. We land into a New York of the late 1990s, a New York somewhere in between the wild urban landscape of the previous generation and the emerging, gentrified New York. It is a globalized playground, either way, for the privileged.

My brother is there. He has emerged from depression to attend NYU for a summer. I crash with him in his dorm. I drink cappuccinos and enjoy the air conditioning. I wander the streets and watch it all.

From New York I travel north, back to the DAPP training center in the Berkshires. We are supposed to spend a couple of months there, reflecting on our experiences or something like that. The truth is that none of us really knows why we are there—other than, perhaps, to be recruited into the Teachers Group. We stay for a few days and break all the rules, then scatter with promises to stay in touch.

I can't go back, can't go to work—I have a job waiting for me at The Children's Center—or see my family. I just need to move. I need to understand now what this place is to which I've returned. America. How is it possible to live in such wealth with such desperate poverty elsewhere? What does it mean to be an American, an abstraction, unmoored, disconnected from place?

My friend Maeve, a peer from Zimbabwe, also isn't ready to return. Home for her is Arizona. She has a girlfriend there and a family who doesn't understand her. I have a car. So, we head north, up through Vermont and into Canada, partying in Montreal, camping in forests dotted with translucent lakes, pondering how we can live in this place among its extravagance and hypocrisy.

Even after I've been back at Sue, I haven't accepted being still. I feel a pull in opposite directions, each something primordial and unavoidable: the community of Sue and the call of the road. In the summer of '99, I get in my car again, first south then north.

I drive through Memphis, which, beyond Beale Street and Graceland is a grimy city, like Rochester, but southern. Poor and depressed. Segregated. I am heading to New Orleans, retracing the steps of the old route of the Great Migration. This takes me through the Delta, where millions of slaves had been taken as cotton became the king of global capitalism. It is here that they remained as second-class citizens long after slavery had been abolished. I camp by a calm little lake, quiet and moonlit. I should be at peace, but I am terrified of the south.

I come to New Orleans before the flood. I walk through all of it. The people don't yet know that they'll be submerged, then banished. It is a sinking city, a memory of the murky, Catholic world it once was, and perhaps, at least in part, still is. After the flood, this will be even less certain.

Like the other American port cities—San Francisco and New York—things are permitted in New Orleans that aren't elsewhere. And its French history makes it different, too. There are blurred lines—Catholic lines—where in the rest of America things are so black and white, so Puritan and dualistic.

And still, this is America. New Orleans is a city that took in slaves from Africa and the Caribbean, from the Virginia and the Carolinas. It brought men, women and children, weeping and brutalized, to feed the global cotton trade. Many of their descendants would make their way to Chicago centuries later, becoming the people I know on the south side. But for those who remain down here, the legacy of slavery is strong, the poverty brutal.

I stay in a youth hostel not far away from the Garden District, where I make friends with Jimmy, a gambler from Key West who is financing this trip by selling guns along the way; and Len, who claims he can train tigers to talk. They are both, in their own way, crazy, both appropriate for New Orleans.

This is before the flood. No one can possibly know what will happen a few years later. We've heard, of course, that New Orleans is at risk, heard that the degradation of the coastal ecosystem and the rising waters and the superstorms of an increasingly hot planet can put New Orleans under water. But the tourists won't care unless their homes end up submerged, too, or unless the people of New Orleans show up in their towns. They come to New Orleans to do things they wouldn't do at home, and leave New Orleans to return to their own towns at higher elevations. This much won't change when the flood comes.

Everyone thinks only of Noah when they think of the flood, not the children who drowned because of their parents' sins.

I travel west, too, to the great empty spaces that, for generations of Americans, have represented freedom. Oklahoma is a vast and empty place, impossibly lonely, it seems to me. I stop in its desolate west at a roadside motel, run by Indians—surprisingly to me, Indians from the subcontinent, not Native Americans. I push westward and camp in the Sangre de Christo Mountains of New Mexico and watch the lightning light up the nighttime sky to the east. I walk through mountain trails and camp in fields of wildflowers, bathe in mountain streams.

I feel lonely and free, and wonder what freedom even is. This is America, the America that I've only ever flown over. It is vast and empty and beautiful. It is possible, here, to be more alone than one could ever be in the coastal cities, or Chicago. Somehow, in the mythology that made this—the "real" America—what it is, loneliness and freedom had become conflated. I am intoxicated by the absolute loneliness of it, not knowing that this is the legacy not only of the American project, but of my own little life, in which loneliness serves as a buffer against the terror of intimacy. The road is beauty, yes, freedom, for sure, but also it is the delusion that protects me from vulnerability.

Somehow, in a land that could only be celebrated and embraced for its beauty, the capitalist extraction of its resources, its uglification and sterility, comes to mean freedom.

I drive on—driving, again, means freedom in America—through the reservations of New Mexico and Arizona. I pick up native hitchhikers who speak little English and who ask me for money when they get out. I remember hitchhiking in Africa, where I, the hitcher, always had to pay.

I drive into the foothills north of the Grand Canyon and camp in pine forest, blissfully alone. The night is terrifying, a constant drum of forest creatures scampering around me. I awake early, shit in a hole and drive off into the Utah desert and on to Las Vegas.

Vegas arises in the desert out of nothing. An oasis, perhaps, or a mirage. But it is real: Sex and gambling and absurd buildings and washed-up celebrities. The casinos blow air conditioning at me as I walk the streets, where women with fake tits beckon me in. I just walk and look. I've come from the desert to this temple of America's religion, capitalism. More than that, Vegas could have been a monument not merely to capitalism—New York perhaps is a better symbol—but also of the hubris that we can transcend nature. Green lawns. Swimming pools. Bright lights. Abundant water. A city of millions. All in a desert that has, for millennia, supported only small bands of humans.

My journey takes me all the way to the Pacific, and I camp up the coast or sleep on old friends' couches. Danny, my old skateboarding buddy, lives in LA, and I crash on his couch, unable to comprehend LA's maze of highways, its absence of humans walking. Patrick lives in Oakland, and we see KRS-1 together in San Francisco. The pacific sunrise is something to behold, and I sit in northern California among the Redwood Groves thinking that I must return to this holy place before it's gone.

10. CHILDREN'S CENTER #2

1998-99

AFTER QUEBEC, I RETURN TO MY JOB AT SUE. I move into a tiny one-bedroom apartment on the lake, in the neighborhood of South Shore. I can see the sun rising over Lake Michigan and hear the gunshots pierce the south side.

When the weather is warm, I walk across the street and leap off the rocks into the lake. Occasionally, lifeguards yell at me that no swimming is permitted. I never can figure out why there are lifeguards if swimming isn't allowed.

This is a different time for me. College is well and truly over. I still go out, still smoke and drink, but far less. Something has changed. I begin to write. My evenings are spent writing and reading in my little apartment with barely any furniture—only a desk and a bare mattress—and no television.

The Children's Center becomes the center of my life—other than my dreams of beyond—and a new family comes that becomes a central part of the community. Ottie and Mattie are sisters who came to Chicago in the 1960s during the Great Migration, leaving behind Jim Crow and sharecropping lives in Arkansas. Ottie is already a grandmother when I meet her, her children grown. But a younger sister—there are perhaps a dozen of them—has become addicted to drugs. Ottie adopts her two children.

This sister keeps having more kids, and now Mattie, another of Ottie's younger sisters, adopts them. They keep coming, keep being born, until Ottie and Mattie each have four children. Each tiny, shivering, and addicted at birth.

But they grow, in body, mind and spirit. They are smart, all of them, even as they carry with them such a weight on their skinny bodies. Traumas of their families, their mother, their ancestors.

Ottie and Mattie teach me the thing in this world that I come to admire more than anything. They make family, community, out of nothing. This is a received wisdom. For centuries this capacity has defined the African American experience. When one loses family, the community takes care.

And I, in a sense, am as much a beneficiary of this gift as those children. It is the closest thing to the miraculous I know.

On Friday evenings I host an open gym for the teens in the neighborhood. My game thrives there, for these are the freest games I've ever played. They are good-natured and joyful, these games, but life on the south side is always on the edge.

A small fight breaks out. No big deal. But one of the kids isn't from the neighborhood. They all jump on him. I barely get the kid out of there alive.

I drive kids home in a big "church van" every night. We stop, that night, in front of a housing project to let a couple of new kids out. A girl, a random girl, maybe 15 years old, gets in the van. "Where we going?" she asks. *Oh shit*, I think. *I am in the projects in a van with a teenaged girl. I am going to get killed. Or arrested.* Eventually she gets out and I race away, not even stopping to close the back door. A burning dumpster has been moved into the middle of the street. I can barely u-turn the mammoth van to head back the other direction.

I stop at the store on my way home. Looking over the nuts and dried fruit in the bulk food section, I notice a woman staring at me, with my long hair and beard. I look at her. She is a slightly older—perhaps in her mid-thirties—Black woman. "You look like a sexy Jesus!" she exclaims, and walks away. I ponder this as I ponder the nuts and dried fruit. There are small things to cling to on the south side of Chicago.

More than ever, I feel like I am a part of a community, a whole community. I have meaningful work. But there is still something that calls me. I have experienced belonging, but still feel the longing. I want to be free, the freedom not of the Vegas desert or New York café, but of the road. I need to suffer more—this is it! I need to feel the planet and its sorrow. Sue has figured out how to do this in a church basement. I need to feel the planet as a whole. I need to walk around the Earth to see if I can make it back. To see if I can feel the texture of the Earth, a sphere, an island floating in the cosmos, our only home. At times, of course, it is the things we most desire that instill in us our greatest fear. Loneliness, that vast and empty sea, only really seems real if we first know belonging. So I run away.

11. THE TWO-INCH GLASS
2000

"Where you going?" the officer says gruffly.

"Division six," I answer blankly.

The officer says nothing. He looks over my documents. He finds no reason to deny my entry.

"You can't enter with this," says the woman to my side who has been searching my bag, holding up an aerosol can.

I take my bag and return to my car, where I leave everything that would prevent me from entering. I return in a few moments, show them my identification card, and resubmit to a search. The officer pats me down after I pass through the metal detector.

"To the right and out the door," he tells me.

This is like entering a foreign country, I think as I walk down the dark corridor. *No, this is more difficult than that. It is like entering a foreign world. It is inside of the world we know, hidden.*

The hallway leads to a door to a courtyard. Not knowing where I am going, I enter the first open door I encounter.

The room is poorly lit and dingy. There are a dozen people sitting in plastic chairs nailed to the floor in neat rows. They do not talk, or read; they stare straight ahead, blankly and sadly, all of them. A woman in uniform sits behind a gate. I can barely see her in the drab and dirty darkness. She asks me whom I have come to see.

I answer, giving a name that feels odd in its formality.

The woman shuffles some papers. "Have a seat," she says, neither kind nor unkind. "Wait for his name to be called."

I sit down among the others. They are a depressing bunch: mothers and fathers; wives and brothers. They have all come to see someone they love who is incarcerated. Their faces are as gray and gloomy as the room.

I wait for about a forty-five minutes. His name is the first to be called. They open a heavy and terrifying iron gate to let me enter. I see Dee to my left as I am led to another room. My identification is scrutinized again. Finally, I am allowed into the visitation room. Dee sits behind two-inch, bulletproof glass, the kind found in hole-in-the-wall fast food places. He is smiling, surprised to see me. His hair has been cut short—he had long dreadlocks the last time I saw him, perhaps a month ago. He looks healthy and strong. He has been eating better there than he ever did when he was free.

In order to talk, we have to put our mouths and ears close to the glass and speak loudly. We make small talk at first. He tells me he has been doing well; he is in good health. In time, more visitors enter, each shouting into the tiny holes in the two-inch glass. It becomes noisy and nearly impossible to hear.

I tell him, after about a half hour, that I have to leave. I won't see him for a while, for I am leaving the country next week. I tell him I will be in Asia. He smiles. I am not sure if he even knows where Asia is; and even if he does know, it is so far beyond his world that it does not matter. It might as well be the moon.

Dee puts his hand up to the glass. I put mine up too, mirroring his. We imagine they touch.

I knew Dee for several years before he was arrested for the murder of his mother. I would see Dee wandering the streets. In time, I come to know him; he becomes a part of my circle of friends.

Hyde Park is one of the South Side's most affluent and integrated neighborhoods. Dee comes regularly to escape the violence of his own neighborhood. There are times when he hears the gunshots on his way home and turns around to sleep in the park; other times he is robbed.

Dee's home fluctuates between the streets and his mother's place. Sometimes he prefers homelessness: his mother is plagued by addiction; his neighborhood is gang-ridden; and his mother's home is rat-infested and unwelcoming. But he harbors no bitterness toward his mother. "She ain't too strong," he tells me once. It is the closest he ever comes to criticizing her in my presence, but it is said with affection. It is an explanation for his mother's problems—an excuse, not a condemnation.

Dee has little formal education and few prospects for employment. Often he comes by hungry—we try to give him what we can. He gets a job selling "Streetwise", a newspaper sold by Chicago's homeless. He sells incense and oils. He is arrested a few times for selling the latter without a license. He would have had to stop eating for several days to afford such a license.

And Dee walks. Through Chicago's harsh and bitter winter, he walks; he walks through Chicago's brutal and violent neighborhoods. Dee crosses borders in Chicago: from one gang territory to another; and from his own poor, Black neighborhood to the white and Black-middle-class neighborhood of Hyde Park. Dee has nothing, but his feet; his only gift, it seems, is his ability to walk these forbidding streets freely.

A few months before I am to leave Chicago, and America, Winston receives a knock on his door. It is the police. They ask him if he knows a man with a long, Biblical-sounding name. He isn't sure. None of us have ever known him by any other name than "Dee". But he figures out who it is.

A few nights ago, Dee's mother was stabbed to death, they tell him. Dee has been arrested.

It is Dee who finds his mother covered in blood. It is no single stab wound that kills her, but a multitude, too many to count. I have thought about how I would have responded if I had been in Dee's situation. My imagination has come up with nothing.

In shock, in horror, Dee does nothing at first. When he regains his composure, he takes the money in his mother's house and leaves. Later, he calls the police.

The police have said that the money was the motive for the crime, that Dee killed his own mother to steal from her. But of course, the truth is always deeper than appearances; or, rather, sometimes, the truth is shallower. The truth is as shallow as a man's clothes and skin. Dee is poor and uneducated, with little chance to defend himself successfully in court; he is big and dark-skinned, fitting society's image of a criminal, a murderer.

I have broken bread with Dee. He has been to my home. I can never have known his innermost thoughts, the depths of his soul. But I know him as more than his clothes and his skin. He is not a shadow, to me, drifting namelessly through the city streets. He is human.

We stand up, for a moment, facing one another. The windowless visitation room is crowded now. On both sides of the divide, mouths and ears are pressed against the two-inch glass. The small room is filled with noise. I am sure no one could hear anything that is said. I have stopped trying.

We say goodbye to each other—this is the word that does not need to be heard to be understood—and I leave. As I leave the building, the guard is arguing with a Mexican kid about his hat. Hats, which represent gang affiliation in Chicago, are not allowed. The August sun shines brightly as I walk away, toward my car. There are no windows inside.

I walk away not only from the Cook County Jail, but also from the darkness, from Chicago, from attachment, from limitation. I am free. I can leave. My imminent departure intensifies, in my own mind, the cruelty of Dee's incarceration.

I will cross so many borders. Most people I know in Chicago, most people I will encounter on my journey, will never cross an international border in their lives.

And there are other borders, more subtle but no less real, that I will be privileged to cross.

It does not yet occur to me then that Dee's existence has always been about crossing borders. He has spent his time with privileged University students. He has walked.

But there, as I get into my car and drive off, I feel the impassibility of the borders of his world now. The two-inch glass does not move. He has no passport, no way to move on, to continue his walk. And I feel the unknowability of him to me, and I to him. This crushes me with sadness.

As I begin my journey, in which I will seldom cease to move, Dee remains static in my mind, always staring out at me, through the two-inch glass.

12. SAMOA
2000

I AM ON FIRE NOW. I need to go, go, go. Late in the summer of the year 2000, I take all my worldly possessions and leave them in storage—a friend's family owns a storage and moving business and lets me do it for free—and leave. My plan, vaguely conceived, is to travel around the world.

I am supposed to start in Fiji. But there is a military coup. A group of indigenous Fijians take over the government run by ethnic Indians. Flights are canceled, travel bans imposed. I read an article, somewhere, about American Samoa. So I go there instead.

I arrive in darkness. From one vast, empty, black infinity to another, I arrive. In the Pacific, like nowhere else in the world, the sea and the sky are mirrors. One emptiness reflecting the other, interrupted only by islands and stars, stars and islands so much the same. At night, the sameness and smallness is accentuated by the black emptiness of sea and sky.

I arrive tearfully and alone, in a smallish, raucous plane of Samoans, the only foreigner. It takes exactly one day, one empty sea, one empty sky, for my bravery to abate. I am alone, afraid. Looking out the window, there is only blackness. Nothing.

I wait, watching the Samoans laugh and talk, happy to almost be home, back from a trip (to see relatives, probably) to the big city, Honolulu. We land, finally. I have been traveling all day, from Chicago to Honolulu, Honolulu to Tutuila, one of the largest planets in the Samoan solar system, in the galaxy of the Pacific.

The islands of the Pacific are so small, so seemingly insignificant, that for thousands of years people have looked up to the great mirror in the sky to find themselves. It is not with any consideration of ancient Polynesian navigators that I first look upwards when I step off the plane; I am simply compelled to do so because I haven't been able to find this little island from the window of the plane. I feel like I am landing nowhere; it is too dark.

I look up, looking for light, looking for God, looking for that sensation I felt on the back of the lorry on Mozambique, wind in my hair. *Freedom*. But freedom from what? This, perhaps, is my *question*. I don't know enough to ask it yet. But if I did, I might understand that I am running away from the things I desire most: intimacy, community, family. Things that, once found, the loss of which will be unbearable. I am looking up to the stars, but find only descent. I am Icarus, falling into the sea.

The others are greeted by family members with *leis*; I stand dumbly as I exit the tiny, open-air airport. I give the taxi driver the name of a hotel I found in a guidebook. He looks at me, slightly puzzled for a moment, then nods, beckoning me into the cab. It is late; we've flown deep into the night. I arrive at what looks like a dingy tiki bar, exchange a few cursory words with the attendant, a muscular guy with no shirt on, while an obese *fa'afafine*—the transgendered who still make a large number in what has become a conservative Christian country—lounges around in the lobby, and go to my even dingier room to try to sleep.

I awake the next day in some version of paradise—the version where there are no resorts or tourists, no white sand beaches. But the sea sparkles. And the people are friendly. I wander around for a few days, unsure of what I am doing or looking for. I find waterfalls, swim in the rocky sea. I'm intensely lonely and exhilarated to be so alone, so far from all I know. I remember.

Stray dogs are a plague. I take to carrying a stick.

There are no tourists in American Samoa, but there is a smattering of ex-pats, white American men, mostly, who've come here to find paradise or to satisfy some fetish. They pick me out quickly, a wanderer, like them. They all want to know what brings me there, and if I am staying. This isn't a place on the way to anywhere, after all. It's only a place that can be the last place—these islands, Polynesia, among the last places on Earth to be settled. They are intrigued when I tell them that I'm not stopping for long, that this is simply a layover on my way to Asia, that I am going to travel around the world. Intrigued, but not understanding. Like me, they are all running from Modernity; but unlike me, they are seeking to rediscover a flat earth, to stop moving. And yet, there is something in the island that was somehow appropriate for the beginnings of my own adventure. For to circumnavigate the globe is to discover that it is, in fact, an island floating in space.

All of Polynesia was colonized by the West, and quickly became something to be used by its colonizers. So small, so distant that it could be imagined to be whatever the colonizer thought. These little islands could be the place for sexual fantasy—I would see this all around me—and then, because of the fantasies of those first Europeans, a place that required proselytizing. The islands are now very conservative, Christian places.

During World War II, the islands were places to stop as the Japanese and Americans bombed the shit out of each other. After the war, when the people with big armies and weapons had rearranged the world to their liking, the islands were divided up accordingly. This meant that some islands, like Tutuila, would be the property of the United States. It meant that they'd still be poor, as before, but that they'd now be sent boxloads of spam to add heart disease to their troubles. It meant that they'd now be a part, more clearly, of the global order. Eventually, the islands of the South Pacific were the site of nuclear tests, tests that still cause birth defects, the extension of the work done underground at the University of Chicago, where I used to pass that statue. This place is, in many ways, the end, the edge, of the world.

So, I am beginning my journey at the end.

In only a few days, I only grow lonelier, and find new lodging at a guesthouse inhabited by a couple of American ex-pats. For the most part, they are in Samoa because of women,

women who are no longer around. They are friendly and helpful, and drive me around the island, taking me to places I won't otherwise encounter. "But if you really want to see the beauty of Tutuila," one of them tells me, "you've got to meet Rory and stay in his cabin."

And so, after five days wandering around the busy, Americanized side of the island, I have Rory pick me up in his truck. He mumbles as we drive around the island, sharing some kava-kava with me. He is from Oklahoma, originally, and claims, falsely, to have lost his accent.

We pull off to the side of the road on the north side of the island. This is dense jungle, incredibly steep hills. Few people live here; those who do are Samoans living a more traditional lifestyle than in Pago-Pago, the main "city" (which is really more of a developed conglomeration of villages). He leads me up a steep trail to a little jungle shack. There is a hose for water, which Rory encourages me to drink. "The only way to build up your immunity," he says. "There are plenty of fruit trees you can eat from," he adds. And he leaves.

The shack is tiny, with a little deck overlooking the sea. A small bed. Old newspaper serves as wallpaper. I am alone.

My days there are spent watching and listening to the jungle. I walk down to the sea to swim, but the rocks and coral are too sharp. Great fruit bats come out in the evening as the stars begin to appear.

I encounter people only once in my days there, a younger man and an older one, who speak little English. They've come to collect young coconuts. The young man climbs a huge palm and tosses them down to the older. They share with me and smile. I return to my awesome loneliness.

Rory returns at the promised date and time and takes me back to Pago Pago. I have time to kill so I go to a beach bar. A chubby Australian surfer serves me drinks and explains how he wound up there on a surfing trip, fell in love, and stayed. I meet a guy from Cleveland who, upon hearing that I am heading to Vietnam, says that there are some Vietnamese girls on the island I should meet—they've been stranded looking for work in a tuna plant. He drives me by the jail where he tosses fruit over the fence to his friend, then searches, in vain, for the Vietnamese girls. I start to get the impression that there is something slimy about this guy and his search for these girls. I have him drop me at the airport early. We are to take a tiny plane across the sea to Apia, Western Samoa, where we can connect with larger planes for flights to Australia and New Zealand.

When we arrive in Apia, we are informed that the flight is delayed. "Want to share a ride to town?" asks an Aussie next to me.

"Sure."

And the Aussie begins to talk.

He travels all over Asia, he explains, installing ATMs. He is now proudly divorced, and it quickly becomes apparent that this was connected to the travel he's done for work. *What else, I think, would a man whose job it is to install ATMs in the world's poorest countries do but fuck prostitutes?*

The prospects for women in Apia are not terrific, apparently. "Too bloody religious," he tells me. But the place is nice. And the lobster is fabulous. He insists on taking me out for drinks and buying me a lobster. I sit and I listen. It is odd. It's as if my three days in the jungle have rendered me incapable of communicating. And, as a result, the Aussie is perfectly content to fill in the blanks.

After sharing a couple of beers at a noisy bar, the Aussie takes me to a restaurant nearby. He pays for everything—the taxis, the beer, the lobster. "Now," he says as we sit down in a quieter setting overlooking the ocean and begin to eat our lobster, "where is it you intend to go?"

I described the path I plan to take, northward through Vietnam and into China, then down through Tibet and into India.

"You're gonna love Vietnam," he tells me with a big grin on his face, chunks of lobster on his lips. "The girls!

"Now, if I were you, I'd skip out on India altogether. Don't know much about China"—evidently, they don't have ATMs there yet—"but India is fucking awful. The smell!" He seems to describe the horrid smell of India with the same gusto with which he described the girls of Vietnam. "And Calcutta." He shakes his head solemnly. "Calcutta is the worst of the worst. The smelliest, dirtiest, most awful place in the world."

What I don't know yet, because I have not yet been around the world, was that this man's job was to flatten the world, to put it on a schedule like the Danish NGO, to remove its texture, its diversity. To make it consumable, like he's done, in his mind, to the girls of Vietnam.

I remain silent. I look out over the Pacific. We'll be heading back to the airport soon, on our way to Asia. One way or another, I think, I must make my way to Calcutta.

Mercifully, and unsurprisingly, my Aussie friend is in first class throughout the flight we share to Sydney. He waves me off ("The Girls!") as I prepare to go through customs for the final leg of my journey to Vietnam.

13. THE FAR EAST
2000

I AWAKE IN A VIETNAMESE HOTEL EXHAUSTED AND DISORIENTED, LIKE I'VE HARDLY SLEPT. I arrived the previous night in the sprawling, chaotic metropolis that is Ho Chi Minh City. I had the foresight to book a hotel—I will be in hostels from that point on—because I figured I'd be a little disoriented when I arrive. And I am.

On a flat map, and in the Western imagination, The Far East is as far from the West as one can get. Aware as I am, in theory, of the absurdity of such an idea, it feels true to me as I wander out onto the Ho Chi Min streets. I walk onto the sidewalk and turn left to the corner, preparing myself to cross. There are no streetlights, no lines. Lanes and signs are mere suggestions. Motorbikes, bicycles and *cyclos* weave among one another. A left turn requires swerving into oncoming traffic.

I stand there, paralyzed, until a man on a *cyclo*—a bicycle rickshaw—approaches. "I take you tour!" he says with a brown-toothed smile. "See beautiful temple!" He pedals me around, showing me the sights, mostly temples, until a fierce tropical downpour comes upon us. He rushes me into a shop where we buy some cokes. He smiles with the few brown teeth he possesses, then shakes his head. "Vietnam," he says with a sad smile. I suppose he means the rain.

I become a frequenter of temples and a connoisseur of "Where the Monks Eat", the ubiquitous Buddhist vegetarian restaurants. These are the only places I can find any rest from the chaotic streets. I revel in and despair at the absolute difference between the place in which I've landed and the place whence I've come.

Vietnam is, for me, inextricably associated with the war. It is here that Tony used his martial skills to their most deadly effect; it is from here that he returned to seek salvation in using those skills to heal. And, of course, there is my father. He spent Vietnam in the Navy, cruising the rivers. Death must have been all around him, but he only ever talked about the hot peppers. He loves hot food, and Vietnam has the spiciest damn peppers he's ever tried, he would tell me.

My time in Ho Chi Minh City is spent wandering the streets, wondering what I was even doing there. I meet no one, speak little. I take one side trip to visit the Cao Dai temple, which mixes Western and Eastern religious traditions. The bus is tiny—I bump my head on the ceiling when I enter. Everyone laughs. I'm followed by a group of ten-year-old-looking girls when I get off and pressured to buy a plastic bag of orange soda. I am ready to give up, but the girls back away and I am able to wander down the country road to the temple complex. *This is Asia*, I think: impossibly green, fields of rice and water buffalo spread out to my left as a river drifts to the right. Everything as I've imagined.

The temple is spectacular. A moving sea of white cloth against the green forest, the worshippers enter together, pray together, and I follow. Then I see them, entering in the back, snapping pictures: a busload of tourists has come.

I take a train north, to Danang, in the center of the country, sharing a room with a father and son. It soon becomes clear that the father is dying. I watch the son massage his father's feet, watch the son spoon mushy food into his father's mouth.

The son wipes his father's mouth gently after each bite as the train passes through the lush countryside. I have no food, but they share what little they have with me.

There is no facility in Vietnam in which to warehouse one's parents. At least none that most can afford. Here, each is blessed and cursed to care for one's dying parents, blessed and cursed to be cared for by one's children.

They get off a few stops before me, returning, I imagine, to their ancestral home where the father will die. They've said nothing the whole way, have given no indication of any affinity. But when they catch my eye from the platform, they smile and wave with what I know is genuine warmth.

I think of Tony, of my father. Of fatherhood and of death. How was my father affected by the war? For a man already disinclined to process his emotions, he would have possessed little to cope with the death and suffering he encountered there. I imagine that he has simply bathed himself in chemical responses, hormonal reactions to allow him to survive, but not really live. And when I couldn't find joy, when I was too angry, perhaps I carried that legacy with me. Perhaps I carry it when I decide, like he did—albeit in a different form—to flee intimacy.

Whatever the reason, as I watch them carry their father from the train, I cannot imagine carrying my own father anywhere as he prepares to die—he would be too heavy, in every way.

I come down with my bag at the train station in Danang, about midway up the Vietnamese coast. My bag is relatively small now—nothing like the "body bag" brought to Spain—but is nothing fancy like that of most of the backpackers I'll encounter. It is an old army bag I bought from a surplus store in Chicago. It isn't the easiest thing to carry, but I figure I'm young and strong and can handle it; and it had the aesthetic I'm seeking. I am living out of this bag, its simplicity a rebellion against the stuff of the modern world.

I am greeted immediately by a man on a motorbike. He introduces himself as Tuan and starts talking fast. He wants to be my guide. At first I resist—"I don't need any fucking guide like a tourist"—but as he speaks, I start thinking how nice it is to have someone speaking English to me. I'm lonely. So I agree.

We ride for days together on his motorbike through central Vietnam, exploring waterfalls, jungles just now growing back from Agent Orange dropped decades ago. He takes me to little restaurants in Danang "where the monks eat", tells me about his family: His family, like so many others, was destroyed by the war—it left him with English at least, which he now uses in his work as a tour guide.

Among the most popular tourist destinations for Americans visiting Vietnam, apparently, is the DMZ, or "Demilitarized Zone." Here, for a small fee, you can see the empty space, denuded still of its foliage, that once separated the north and south. You can enter the tunnels that the Viet Kong dug to avoid the US bombs. They dug holes, like I did behind my garage as a kid, like the ancient cave people at Altamira. But they were simply trying not to die. The war ended with that border being eradicated while other borders were built—geopolitical borders, cold war borders; and also borders in the minds of those the war left behind, borders much harder to breach.

I tell Tuan I'm not interested in the DMZ, only waterfalls and temples. I don't tell him about Tony or my father.

War, it seems, is a gift and a trauma that goes beyond those who fight. This Buddhist country—and it is thoroughly Buddhist in spite of the communist rule and the smattering of Catholic Churches left by the French—understands this, understands the karmic relationships that pass trauma on from husbands to wives, fathers to sons. It seems that even Tuan and I are connected, absurdly, awesomely, through the memory of war. In Vietnam they call it the American War; in America they call it the Vietnam War. How much closer can two countries be, in spite of all the distance and difference? It is like how a father can pass on a past hurt to a son through his silence, the gift, like war, of patriarchy.

Tuan leaves me at the train station as I get ready to head north to Hanoi, where I will spend several uneventful days—riding my bike past the infamous hotel Hanoi, throughout its streets, much quieter and cleaner than Ho Chi Minh City's—before moving on to China. Hanoi is a beautiful city, with French architecture and dotted with lakes and pagodas. In front of the train station in Danang, Tuan and I speak of crime in Vietnam and the US. He understands that in Vietnam there is far less. But it's becoming more of a problem, he explains, especially drugs. "I think that anyone who is caught with drugs should be executed," he tells me. "This would solve the problem." I can only nod and say goodbye. I have a train to catch.

Guilin is gray and boring. Industrial, like so much of the urban China I will encounter. I have arrived there from a long but not altogether unpleasant train ride from Hanoi. I find a bus to Yangshuo—more of a van, really—and sit down. I am alone in my row. Others get on, eventually filling the other rows until only seats next to mine are available. An argument breaks out. I speak no Chinese, but it doesn't take long for me to figure out that they are arguing about *me*. No one wants to sit next to a foreigner. Eventually, a smiling man in a suit gets up from his own seat and offers to sit with me. I think of him as a businessman because of his clothes. He smiles at me and begins to speak broken English. He is learning, he explains, and this could be practice for him. His kindness is remarkable.

This is my introduction to China, modern China. The China that is so different from the China of my imagination, of bagua. It is a place poised between its isolation from and unique place in the global order—the reality for China is that in its rejection of Western Capitalism it has always embraced Western notions of progress and materialism while rejecting its own past. What is China now? Its defining feature, for me, is murky—literally. It is a place choking on its own contradictions. Literally.

Yangshuo, where I take the van to from Guilin, is a shitty backpacker town. The only thing like it in all of China. Backpackers love the place. I hate it. I will learn later, as I travel throughout the country, that there is really nowhere else in turn of the century China so foreigner-friendly in China. So this is part of the appeal. In Yangshuo, I can drink beer with loudmouthed Brits and Aussies who don't give a shit about China—this is their gap-year adventure and nothing more.

But there is a reason Yangshuo is the place backpackers come to be with each other. It is Old China, before the smokestacks and smog—even before Mao. I rent a bike each day and ride through the countryside, passing rice-patties and steep, low mountains that look as if they've been thrust into the Earth by the gods. Men and women live as they have for centuries here, even in caves.

I meet no one, speak little.

After a few days I get on a train in Guilin and head north. The train will be the place where I'll find the best opportunities to meet the Chinese—for whatever reason, the Chinese on the streets are unfriendly, but on the train they are quite welcoming. It feels like being in someone's living room—men change clothes; women prepare tea.

A group of women notices me, the foreigner, traveling alone, and begin, in a straightforward but not unfriendly way, to ask what I am doing and where I am going. In the course of the friendly interrogation, they gather that I am an American, traveling alone, who doesn't know any Chinese. They are worried.

One woman, younger than the rest, speaks some English and emerges as their spokesperson.

"Where you go?" she asks.

"Zhengzhou," I declare. I say it in a way—with a total lack of self-awareness—that reveals my American sense of I-can-go-anywhere-I-want. No Chinese would have said it this way.

She looks back at me. She is hard to read, but I sense disapproval. "You go alone?"

"Yes."

She turns and explains to the others. I have no idea what she says, but it is easy to deduce that she is telling them that this lunatic/idiot is traveling alone to Zhengzhou. The others started talking at once.

"I help," she says.

Her name is Hwang, and she tells me she will take care of me while I stay in the Zhengzhou area. Zhengzhou isn't really much of a destination, but a place to stop while visiting Shaolin Temple and Kaifeng nearby. There are no youth hostels, no backpackers in Zhengzhou. But there is a hotel next to the train station that has an annex with cheap rooms—windowless cells with a shared, foul-smelling bathroom. Hwang leaves me there and says she'll return the next day to take me wherever I want.

For the next few days, Hwang is my tour guide. She shows me the sites of downtown Zhengzhou, which consists of a mall and pollution, a few tall buildings. Many people. We go to Shaolin temple and Kaifeng, places that are most notable to the extent that they are closer to the foreign imagination of China than the reality. The real, present-day China is what I awake to each morning with the cacophony of phlegm, which I would then join, spitting out the black filth I breathed in the previous day; it is new development and business; it is the simultaneous leap into the global economy and the fear of the stranger.

I find in Kaifeng, if only briefly, a respite from the smog and the crowds. But I never really find the old China of my imagination. China once created a world of harmony. Yin and Yang balanced in cosmos and in the human—microcosm and macrocosm. It situated the human in relationship, and brought forth a cosmos in which change was fundamental. It is said that one-thousand years ago, the Chinese viewed a supernova in the heavens that was unreported in the West; for them, change was expected, whereas in the West, we were blinded by our assumption that the stars in the heavens were fixed. But now, somehow, it seems that the assumptions of the places I left are shared here, too. Industry and progress are the virtues of the new China, and the people are choking on it.

On my final day in Zhengzhou, Hwang asks me, "You go 'Tibet'?"

I say that I am.

"Some people say Tibet is separate country from China," she says. Then pauses. "Tibet is ours."

The first thing you notice when traveling to Tibet from China is the clear air. Beyond the city there seems to be an immense nothingness, an expanse of clear, cool air that goes on forever. Nonetheless, each morning I am awakened by the same snorting and coughing and spitting that brings up the black mucus from my neighbors' lungs.

Tibet, unlike China, remains devoutly Buddhist, and its rhythms are dictated by temple and monk. Lhasa has only been moderately sinicized. But its culture is increasingly under siege. More and more Chinese will move there, displacing Tibetans and Tibetan culture.

Here, the youth hostels are more abundant and friendlier than in China, and I manage to meet fellow travelers. And these travelers are a bit more adventurous than those one might meet in places like Thailand. Tibet is not for the timid, or for the beer swilling Westerner.

I meet Sergio in the courtyard at the hostel eating some Muesli with a quiet and serious Dane—I recognize the character from my days in Zimbabwe. Sergio is shouting across the courtyard to a young woman who works at the hostel. "I am going to make you my girlfriend!" He is shouting repeatedly. Periodically he turns to us to say, "But first she needs to brush her teeth!"

Sergio is from the island of Ischia, just off the coast of Naples. He's traveled the world, even more than I have. There are stories of eating cockroaches in Papua New Guinea, of motorcycle rides across Africa, and, most proudly, of his encounters with the Chinese police in Tibet.

Sergio is a performer, an actor playing himself in a bio-pic. He is neither an intellectual nor a hippie. And he isn't a kid on some gap year journey. Back home, Sergio lives a prosperous but provincial life in the south of Italy where his family runs a prominent interior design business.

Everywhere Sergio goes he performs with a smile. He loudly mocks the Tibetans even as he scorns the oppressive Chinese authorities. It isn't so much that he cares about the politics. For Sergio, the issue is the limits the Chinese place on travelers. When he first came to Tibet, he flouted the restrictions placed on foreigners and got on a local bus. He was quickly identified and arrested. As he describes it, he was interrogated by a harmless buffoon who asked him a bunch of mundane questions about his travels. Sergio simply smiled and pretended to be confused.

"What kind of work do you do in Italy?" asked the policeman.

"Interior decorating."

The policeman seemed not to believe him. "OK. So, if you were going to redesign this office, what would you do?"

Sergio then went into such an expansive and detailed response that the policeman became convinced he should redesign the office. He was let go with a small fine and a list of office design ideas.

Another night he is nearly caught trying to cut down the Chinese flag in front of Potala Palace. This time he is drunk and has to run off.

Sergio is a bargainer—a common practice in most of the world, and a complex and nuanced practice for the Western traveler. When you travel from a wealthy country to a poor one, everyone sees this and jacks up the prices. It can be infuriating. At the same time, you also might feel that it's only fair to pay a little extra. But you have to be careful not to be marked as an easy target for scams. Each traveler has to navigate the morality of this equation—an equation that is never equal. Sergio doesn't do the nuance. He negotiates everything, no matter how cheap, and refuses to pay "foreigners' prices". I once saw him talk down a bartender on the price of a beer because the glass was chipped. He claims that his penchant for negotiation comes from the family business in which, the day after an estimate is proffered, a prospective client will invariably come to the office with a list of deaths and other family hardships in hopes of a better deal.

When I meet Sergio, he has given up on traveling across Tibet like a local and is ready to do it the way the Chinese mandate: hiring a car and driver. We agree to be partners and begin to find a group to share the costs.

In the meantime, I am spending my days biking around Lhasa, visiting temples and seeing the sites. I feel reasonably good, but there is no doubt that I am feeling the effects of altitude: slightly short of breath, slightly weary. But I figure I'll be fine.

I meet a Tibetan guy and British backpacker one afternoon in the market in Lhasa. I feel short of breath that day, but think nothing of it. This is considered normal in Tibet, after all. We begin to talk and wander into the courtyard of the guesthouse where the Englishman is staying. And then I am falling. Falling from the highest country on Earth, the Himalayan heights of Tibet, down into a pile of rocks. I am Icarus again. Falling. I had thought I could leave, touch the sun.

The next thing I know they are pulling me to my feet, blood pouring down my face. I've fainted and smashed my head on a rock.

"Oooohhh!" wails the Tibetan. "It looks awful."

They give me a rag to put over my eye to stem the bleeding, but it quickly becomes clear that I'll need stitches. "We need to take you to a doctor," says the Englishman. I nod, stunned, in agreement.

"It looks so bad," exclaims the Tibetan again. "He's right. Follow me." And we grab a rickshaw to the nearest hospital.

The "hospital" in Lhasa is not much to speak of. A couple of rooms. A couple of guys—the doctors, I presume—sitting around, looking bored. They usher me into a room and help me onto a table.

"He needs stitches," says the Englishmen. The Tibetan repeats in Tibetan and in a somewhat more panicked tone. I nod along with the doctor. He fumbles through some drawers, then leaves. We sit there silently for a while. The Englishman is calm, the Tibetan pacing. Every now and then he mutters something about the awfulness of my injury.

"Where did they go?" I ask.

"Oh," says the Tibetan, "he couldn't find the key to the drawer where they keep the clean needles."

"I'll wait," I say. In America, clean needles are everywhere; everything is sterile. Here, flies buzz around the food at the market and everything is covered in dust. They have to look for the clean needles because, it seems, nothing is clean. And yet, somehow, this means that everything is also alive in a way that it isn't in America.

They come back shortly and stitch me up. It is clear now that I am suffering from altitude sickness. The only real cure, of course, is to go to a lower elevation. But here, on top of the world, there is nowhere to go. I can only wait and rest and do what most of the world in most of history has done in sickness: pray. And I do.

Wait and rest. It is the opposite impulse of the constant movement of the traveler. But it is far more consistent with the Buddhist practices of Tibet. Sit and wait and breathe.

This is the practice. It is what I, the out-of-breath American, need to do, and find it hard to do. It is through this breathing that the central insight of Buddhism comes to light: This identity to which we cling, to which we are so attached, is illusory. *Anatman*. No Self. It doesn't mean we don't exist. Rather, it means that we only exist in *relationship*. When I start to think of who I am, I find myself unable to isolate myself from anyone or anything. I am enmeshed in a web of interrelatedness. The planet is round; we depend on each other. Some of us cannot breathe because we cannot be still; others of us cannot breathe because someone else has poisoned the air, because someone else has made a murderous decision on the other side of the globe.

Finally, a few days later, we leave Lhasa. I believe I am largely over my illness. We ride out on a tarred road that quickly turns to dirt, a dusty expanse across the Tibetan plateau. Dust seeps into our Range Rover as we listen to Bob Marley and cover our mouths, choking on the dust. The Tibetan plateau stretches out before us, impossibly immense and empty and bright. We are off into an occupied land, a land that the Chinese government has attempted to turn Chinese through the magic of language; by simply *naming* it something Chinese, Tibet will *become* Chinese.

There are seven of us squeezed into the Range Rover: Sergio and I; a Canadian couple; Chin, a Malaysian Buddhist nun; and the driver and guide. The guide is a sort of joke to us all.

He shares no common language with any of us and seems to have little to offer in the way of guidance. It just appears to be another bureaucratic measure from the Chinese government.

Our first stop is Samye Monastery, a temple complex about a day's drive from Lhasa. The temple can only be reached by boat, and we leave our car and take a small craft across the river. The Tibetans scoop water from the river and drink it as Sergio films with his camcorder. "Look at them drink the dirty water!" He narrates gleefully.

The boatman removes his shoes, but not his socks, to get out into the water as we reach the other side. Sergio, still filming, declares: "Look at how stupid this guy is! He's wearing socks in the water!"

By the time we reach the temple, I've become sick again. I'm nauseous and short of breath, as if I am drowning. But the temple is comfortable, and I am able to rest and recover. My stomach still feels uneasy—not ideal for another long drive—but I can make it. There is no choice; there is nowhere else to go. It will be days before we'll descend into a valley.

Our travels through Tibet consist of stops in small towns and temples. We walk through the temples—Chin, Sergio, and I, led by our silent guide (the Canadians declare themselves to be tired of temples)—listening and watching.

The monks are young men, teenagers mostly, and seem interested in engaging foreigners. They come across as happy teenagers rather than stoic monks. In one temple, Sergio decides to make things interesting and challenges the biggest monk to an arm-wrestling match. "You," he says, pointing to the monk and sitting down at a table with the universally understood posture of the arm wrestle, "come on." When Sergio wins—the biggest monk isn't terribly big—he tears off his shirt, leaps on a huge vat of yak butter tea, and flexes.

We ride on through the dust, slowly, staring at the mountains in the distance and squinting in the vast clarity of the sun-soaked plateau. As we approach the Himalayas, the air grows even thinner and colder. I've recovered from the worst of my illness, but I am still weak and have little appetite. This isn't such a bad place to lack an appetite—the menu is limited.

Our second to last evening before Everest base camp was in a little village called Tashi Dzom. I sit in a bar with Sergio, Chin, and a local man who speaks English, debating the relative merits of vegetarianism and Buddhism. Sergio speaks of Francis, Chin of her Malay Buddhism, the stranger of Tibetan Vajrayana Buddhism.

When we have finished, we walk out into the street. It's dusk, and we stand awestruck on a single dusty road through a little town that seems even smaller because of the vastness of the plateau to the east, west, and north, and the immensity of the Himalayas to the south. Everest rises up above us in the distance. The people follow us from the tavern, and soon we find ourselves surrounded by the village children. They carry instruments and sing and dance. It's unclear if they dance and sing for us, just as it is unclear if the Himalayas have risen up out of the Earth for us—a slower dance but a dance nonetheless. In the end, it doesn't matter. They dance on the dusty road as if to say that although this may be a messy, dirty, poor land, it is alive. They rise up, like Everest, the texture of the planet.

We ride on to the next village, nestled in a canyon that leads to Everest base camp. Our accommodation is the home of a Tibetan family, who feeds us and provides us with an unheated room filled with warm blankets. We sleep well. One of the Canadians who's trained as an EMT removes my stitches.

I awake early, in the darkness. I have to shit. The pit toilet is outside, and uncovered. The air is bitter cold and clear. I squat and look up. The stars are so close that it seems I could touch them.

Everest base camp is reachable only by foot, a walk that takes a couple of hours from the end of the road. Sergio, Chin and I walk together, discussing whether or not the majestic

Himalayas, the dancing children, and us have come to being through karmic relationships or through God's blessings. The matter will remain unsettled.

Sergio and I are so different, but it seems that we are both doing the same thing. Running away. Looking for something that can never be found until we stop looking.

The descent from the Tibetan plateau is one of dryness into moisture, desert into jungle, sparseness into fullness, Buddhism into Hinduism, simplicity into chaos. The Himalayas are a border, a real border, between two worlds. I can feel the wetness in the air, feel the rich air in my lungs as we drive down into the borderlands. I have been, in Tibet, in the Himalayas, on top of the world. I touched the sky, and it nearly killed me. Now, I descend.

14. THE SUBCONTINENT
2000

I'M ON A BUS HEADING INTO INDIA WITH A GROUP OF LOUD AND CLIQUISH ISRAELIS. Such groups are common on the subcontinent, generally having come there after a stint in the army. In India, they can smoke hash and forget about their last couple of years manning Palestinian checkpoints. They always travel in groups and don't tend to mix much with the other backpackers. This group is no different. Nepali roads are brutal, meandering, twisted and bumpy through the Himalayas, and the traveling is always slow. Sometimes the road is barely passable. At one point someone is hit and killed on the road ahead of us. An Israeli leaps to his feet and runs onto the road to try to save him—presumably he's had some kind of training in the IDF—but the man dies anyway.

In time we navigate the mountains and the roads straighten out, long and flat, as we race towards the border. When the bus lets us out, the Israelis scatter and I am left standing in the chaos and begin to walk in the direction I assume to be India. I walk and walk, and soon realize that I am, in fact, already in India. I've passed the border without getting my passport stamped. I walk back and eventually find the little stall that is the office. They stamp my passport and I walk back out onto the street.

Cows and shit and incense and people, everywhere, assault my senses. Beggars harass me. I find myself standing next to Pierre, a Frenchman. He's chatty and looking for a friend. I notice that his backpack has a huge padlock on it.

He's been to India before and knows this border well. He's eager to teach me. Borders, he explains, are filled with criminal activity. They are the primary place where one might get robbed, and therefore one has to be particularly careful at the border. And in India, he explains, everyone is looking to scam you or rob you. I nod as we walk.

"Where are you going?" he asks.

"Varanasi," I answer. "But I probably won't make it much further than Gorakpur today. I know that's the closest place to catch a train."

"Gorakpur," he spits. "It's an awful place."—It *does* have that reputation—"Let's hope we don't spend much time there. Come on. Let's find the bus. I will negotiate. They always try to rob you with these bus tickets."

Pierre and I walk a bit to the crowded bus terminal, where we find a bus heading to Gorakpur. It's full, so they put us on the roof. Pierre is terrified; I am exhilarated. In this particular case, he is probably the wiser. But before we get too far, the police stop the bus, waving their batons, forcing us down. They tell the driver we'll have to ride inside or not at all. They stuff us into the bus, hot and exhausted, where we'll ride standing up into the night.

I watch out the window as the sun sets across the Ganges plain, as men squat in field after field, shitting in the open.

In the dark, clearly not at our destination, the bus pulls off the road. I stand on the side of the road next to Pierre for a while, and we eventually figure out that the bus is having engine trouble. They are trying to fix it.

"Let's try to hitch a ride," I say.

He doesn't like the idea. This feels dangerous.

After a little bit of back and forth, I tell him that I'm going with or without him. I'm not going to wait in the dark for them to fix this bus. I walk to the side of the road and put my hand up. Reluctantly, he follows.

It takes little time to find a ride. A jeep pulls over and tells us how much they'll charge to take us to Gorakpur. It isn't a lot, so we agree. The jeep is nearly full. There is enough room for me to put one buttock on the seat while the other hangs off into wind. Pierre sits on my lap. We drive full speed into the dark night. There are no streetlights, only the lights of cars. The horn blares as cows and humans dive out of the way.

Finally, Gorakpur. Its reputation is well deserved. It is incredibly filthy and hot. The insects are Paleolithic in both size and quantity. We find a cheap hotel—we each get a closet-sized room with a large, insect-plastered window and AC for about a dollar.

The train station is a mass of people and livestock. Stray dogs growl at us but don't come too close. Cows wander and shit. People are lined up, families and extended families, in long rows to sleep on the platform. We get in "line"—more a collection of people pushing one another—and, when we finally get to the front, have to contend with people reaching around us, pushing and yelling. "It's not nice!" shouts Pierre. "It's not right!"

There are no lines in India, no queues, no boundaries between human and animal space, between sleeping and eating space, between public space and toilets.

Finally, we get the tickets and eat cheap and delicious food at an outdoor café, swatting away the insects. My train to Varanasi is early, before Pierre's, who is on his way to Delhi. I will never see him again.

As the sun rises, I watch out across the Ganges plain. More shitting in the wheat fields. The chai wallah comes—"Chachaaaaaaaiiiiiiiii!"—a legless boy who never makes eye contact, conveying wordlessly his absolute submissiveness as he scurries down the aisle. The ubiquitous chai masala, "mixed tea," the sweet, spicy, milky drink that one finds everywhere.

This is India. Mixed. A place where lines seem always blurry, where it seems that everything mixed together. The smells— the smells! There is nothing like the smells of India—of shit and incense assault the nose; beggars and billionaires pass one another on the streets. The traditions of the culture were never as absolute and singular as in the monotheistic traditions to the West. One cannot really even speak of Hinduism—it is really Hinduisms.

In Varanasi, one might encounter worshippers of Vishnu, through Ram or Krishna, perhaps, or of Shiva. All is called "Hinduism". Its most sublime flowering came through Vedanta. But at the same time, there was an elitism to the Vedantic tradition. It isn't entirely for the masses. In India, the lines of caste are the only lines that seem unbreakable. In

India, the notion that lines are blurry is itself even blurry, for some lines are as rigid here as anywhere.

Varanasi is like a city from my dreams of India, a city of seekers, Indian and foreign, New Age and ancient. All that is required is to walk its tangled streets. I arrive at midday and quickly find a hostel—here, as in most parts of India, there is always someone ready to offer guidance, a tour guide, a place to stay—for a price. There is no time to adjust in anonymity. I am dragged into temples, a red dot painted on my forehead; children hound me for money and food; men carry the dead through the city on their way to the river, where bodies are floated down to paradise, past fisherman, past bathers, playful children and pilgrims alike, purified in its filth. India.

Since I met the ATM-installer in Samoa, I have known I had to go to Calcutta. So, from Varanasi I take a train there. The train station, like all Indian train stations, is a masala-mix of all that India is. There is shit everywhere—human, cow, dog. Families sleep and bathe on the platform.

I arrive with a mild cold and take a couple of days sweating and recovering in my dingy hostel. My plan is to volunteer with street children at the Missionaries of Charity, the organization of Mother Theresa.

There, nuns care for children who have been rescued from the streets. These are children with severe disabilities. They come with missing and disfigured limbs, broken bodies and minds. And a group of volunteers cares for them and attempts to, in some small way, make their lives better. Some of the volunteers have been there for months and really know what to do with the children. I struggle.

In the streets of Calcutta, there is always a beggar nearby. I am amazed at how entire families line the streets. People piss and shit in the open, men shave and bathe on sidewalks. Rickshaws pulled by hand. Packs of children follow me, looking for money or food. I occasionally give them something, but in time I learn, as I did in Africa, to disengage or I'll attract a pack. I question why I don't give them everything. But I still give nothing. One beggar stalks and harasses me each day as I leave the mission.

Without any particularly useful skills or the natural bubbliness that some have with these kids, I am given a specific and rudimentary task. The nuns routinely shave the heads of children due to the plague of "animals"—their word for lice—in their hair. The children—for some because they didn't understand what was happening, for others because they really couldn't control their bodies—have to be restrained. This becomes my job. Day after day, I am to hold the confused and terrified children as the nun shaves their heads.

One day, Fergy, the Duchess of York, arrives for a visit. I watch the nuns line up now, like the children lining up to have their heads shaved (but giddy with excitement rather than scared), as she smiles and poses for photos with the bald and broken children.

I shave my head, too. In solidarity, maybe, or perhaps fear of lice, or perhaps in anticipation of something new.

I am lonely and feel only the need to push on. Jagannath Temple, the site of the annual festival in which a great Vishnu avatar, Jagannath, smiling and wide-eyed, is pushed through the streets like a great steamroller, even plowing over devotees in his blind path. It is from this that the British came up with the word "juggernaut". Jagannath is all that India is: complex, masala, syncretic, loving, fierce. But I find no welcome. I am chased from the temples, mocked on the buses in languages I can't understand. I'm growing tired of the chaos, the constant assault of beggars and touts. I couldn't feel lonelier: But I am a juggernaut, like Jagannath. I am unstoppable, and keep on moving, blindly.

And there is the majestic and serene Taj Mahal, a dedication from a Mogul king to his deceased bride, a testament to love. A symbol of a Hindu nation built by a Muslim king, in a country now plagued by Hindutva fundamentalism, the descent into fascism. In a crowded and dirty city, it is an oasis of calm. Its vast stone floor somehow cooler than the rest of the place. It is like an upside-down teardrop, rising out of the Indian Earth, just as India itself is something like a great teardrop, falling from the Himalayas.

I am something like a seeker in India, although I don't want to end up at any ashram. So I travel north, to Rishikesh, a town upstream on the Ganges, toward the mountains, known as a place where Westerners can study yoga and Vedanta. I also know it will be less congested.

I always take the train second-class, but this time I accidentally enter the third-class train. It's dark and smells like people, that deep and ancient smell we've nullified in the new and sterile world. I almost gag. I realize, quickly, that I am in the wrong car, but people are pushing on behind me. I have to push back to get out. I stumble over a man sitting on the floor. He yells at me. Finally I stagger off, breathlessly.

My ride in second class is better, but hardly comfortable. It is an overnight train and I have a bed, but people start wandering in from third-class and join me in my bed. It's bitterly cold. As the sun rises in the Himalayan foothills, I get up to stick my head out the door, catching what little warmth I can get from the sun.

Rishikesh is a little town built along the Ganges. Half of it is only accessible by foot, across a footbridge monitored closely by a band of monkeys—if they sniff any food, they'll leap down to take it. Further along, I encounter humans dressed as monkeys—devotees of Hanuman—who may also screech, but at least won't take your food.

After a quiet couple of days, a Sadhu approaches me and asks, "What are you looking for?"

I stare at him, unsure how to respond.

"Come," he says, "we drink tea. We talk."

His name is Shiva Balek, and he declares himself to be my spiritual teacher—or something like that. He mostly teaches me mantras in Sanskrit, offering little in the way of explanation. He does, however, consistently ask for money. "I am not feeling well today," he might say, "I've been drinking holy Ganga water and it is bothering my stomach. I need money for medicine."

After a few days, I grow tired of this. I leave for Haridwar, another town known as a spiritual center, but less accommodating to foreigners. I stand out in the evening as candles are placed in the Ganges. Each candle represents a wish, granted when it floats down—for the luckiest—to the sea, where it returns to its source, like the soul after death—for the luckiest. This is India: Dead bodies and garbage and wishes, all floating in the same river, honest and deceitful, hideous and beautiful. *Masala*. It is India's radical pluralism that gives it its texture, its taste, like its curries and its tea. Its philosophies, however, point us from the murky river to the sea, from diversity to unity. It embraces this, and other, paradoxes.

India understands that to fall in love with the whole—with God—without knowing and loving the messy particulars, is mere abstraction.

My final destination in India is Amritsar, the site of the Golden Temple, the Sikhs' holiest place. It is also close to the only border crossing into Pakistan. The Sikhs of the Punjab are a border people, neither Muslim nor Hindu, at times shunned by both.

Here, in the Golden Temple, they will provide food and shelter for anyone who asks. I sleep there in the temple complex—there is a special room for foreigners—and eat lentils and naan with the multitudes, and prepare to enter the Muslim world.

The border between India and Pakistan is one of the loneliest I've ever been to. A long and dusty road, stretching out from India's chaotic mixture, its many gods, to the singularly focused Islam of Pakistan. The border guard must be bored—almost no one crosses here—so he gleefully decides to search me. He's convinced I am bringing alcohol into Pakistan and repeatedly asks me about it with an annoying smirk, looking for *baksheesh*.

This border has the tensions that come with hostility, with histories of violence. The partition, the great parting gift from the British Empire to India, left behind a trail of displaced and murdered people. In its wake, what was once a pluralistic, multicultural India became a place in which faith and identity are intertwined. Hinduism—a thing that really never existed until outsiders felt compelled to name it—became conflated with Indianness. I've passed temples built on the ashes of mosques, heard stories of massacred Muslims. Of course, the Muslim side, into which I am traveling, has been transformed by partition, too. What was once an Indian Islam, a Sufi Islam, is slowly being replaced by a more global and fundamentalist Islam. In the age of globalism, everything has to be only one thing. But to be only one thing leaves me wondering how one could even be Indian—how one could be anything but cog in the capitalist machine. Pakistan, like India, has nuclear weapons. It wants to be at once a modern, capitalist state and also fundamentalist, somehow crafting an identity that stands against India, against the West, and also embrace its core values, its hard and immovable fundamentalist lines.

From far away, I read the headlines of unrest to the west, in another land of absurd borders and barbed wire fences and bombs: Ariel Sharon has entered al-Aqsa Mosque; the Second Intifada has erupted in Palestine.

I ride a bus into the city with a metal partition to separate men and women. All the women are completely covered—I will scarcely encounter any women during the whole time I am there. The muezzin cries out the call to prayer: *ALLAAAAAAAH U AKBAR*. I find a cheap and spacious room and settle in.

Lahore is a not-altogether-unpleasant place to be. And I am stuck there for a while: I need a visa to enter Iran and have to wait until I get one through the consulate there. It is congested and chaotic like India, but has a different feel. Pakistan, having been forged out of the brutal partition, is as Islamic a place as I'll ever visit. There are almost no non-Muslims in the country. And it is an increasingly fundamentalist version of Islam, exported from the Gulf States. Its traditions of Sufi mysticism and pluralism are being marginalized. Modernity on one side and fundamentalism on the other are squeezing the mystics out.

The streets are dirty and crowded, filled with auto-repair shops. But they are mellow, in a way, compared to the Indian streets. There is no begging. And it is Ramadan, so most spend long periods of the day resting and waiting for sunset.

I meet Javed walking these streets. He just sort of sidles up next to me and begins to speak. "I am practicing my English," he explains. He is a middle manager sort, or a low-level bureaucrat—I can't gather which. Smart, fairly educated, conservative by Western standards but Westernized. We speak of America—always the thing people want to know—and of family, of religion. My answer, well-rehearsed, is that I am seeking to learn more about Islam. He is devout, disapproving of the Sufism that was his country's practice for centuries.

He invites me to see his home. We wander through labyrinthine alleys, increasingly narrow, until we reach his door. I'm told to wait outside while he "prepares". I just then notice, as I wait, the heroin addict slumped in a corner. I suppose I should be a little cautious, but I'm not. Javed is just so earnest, with his buttoned-down shirt tucked in.

"Come in," he calls with a smile as his head appears in the window. Children run about in a cramped space, made smaller by the tapestry that has been hastily put up in the middle of the room.

"I had to put this up so you would not see my wife," he explains apologetically. "It's not that I would really care. But the families..."

I nod, believing him. He seems embarrassed by the piety, knowing that an American would never do such a thing and, perhaps, would think it backward. I can't help but feel embarrassed for him. While I don't exactly approve, I don't judge him for this, either.

He goes on about his marriage, arranged through the families. "I never got to see her face until we were married," he continues. "But when I did I was so happy! So relieved! Her skin was so light!"

Lahore is a maze of dust and smoke, of men and only hints, apparitions, of women. I can't help but enter into the rhythms of Ramadan. The muezzin wakes us every morning before dawn. Everyone, at this time, prays and eats a huge meal in order to last until sunset. I fast, too. There seems like nothing else to do.

My mission in Lahore to obtain a visa to get into Iran is no small task for an American. I return to the consulate again and again and am told to wait again and again. They aren't unfriendly, calling me "The American". After being told to wait another week for a response, I decide that I need to leave Lahore.

I choose Multan because of its association with Sufism. It proves to be a challenging place to visit, so I leave again for the countryside, but I get horribly sick from the food, and end up in a hospital in nearby Bahawalpur. I think I might be dying, but when they put me in a large room filled with beds—they offer me my own room because I am a foreigner, but I refuse—I am able to see just how sick one can get. I am not dying.

I am drawn to Sufism for the same reason that I am walking around the Earth. It is the lesson that I keep struggling to learn. In Islam, the notion of *Tawhid* is generally taken to mean the unity of God. That is, one shouldn't attribute divinity to anyone or anything but God. In fundamentalist Pakistan, there is a lot of energy devoted to getting rid of practices, like Sufism, that are accused of doing this. In Sufi traditions, *Tawhid* is understood somewhat differently—or at least in a more nuanced way. Rather than "there is no god but God," it is "there is no *thing* but God." There is nothing that does not have a little bit of God in it. Forgetting this is the great sin. Remembering this, but not losing the uniqueness of each person, each place, each being, each moment is the great task.

Finally, the visa has come through. I can go to Iran, they tell me, but I will need to sign up for a "tour." Don't worry, they explain, I can abandon the tour bus whenever I want, as long as I can prove that I've signed up, I'm approved. He makes a call and a couple of guys who speak flawless English come pick me up in an auto-rickshaw. They take me to their office. We talk about how Islam is viewed in the West. I pay them and I'm off, to the west.

Quetta, in the tribal areas of western Pakistan, is nothing like the Pakistan I've come to know. It is dry and mountainous. There is space here. There's a wildness to the place. I am in central Asia now, not the subcontinent. Men ride through town on the backs of pickups with AK-47s strapped to their backs. This is only a few miles—and culturally indistinguishable—from Taliban-controlled Afghanistan. This is where the extremism of fundamentalist Islam is strongest, where it has become a force of death, a cultural deprivation for millions. What we are told in the West is that our way of life is the remedy—that all these people need are more televisions, more capitalism. Better shopping. But capitalism is more cause than cure. Fundamentalism here as elsewhere—India, for example, or a megachurch in Illinois—is a *response* to Modernity. It's nothing more than Prozac—something to avoid the feeling of not having a place in the world.

I'm regularly invited for tea in Quetta and appreciate the hospitable climate, the spaciousness. This is the other side to Islam. Nowhere, other than rural Africa, has been friendlier to me, more welcoming. But this is only a stopover. After the wait, I am eager to move on to Iran.

It is an overnight bus to the border, through the desert, an uncomfortable ride, cramped and—after sunset when smoking is permitted—smoky. We pass camel caravans in the night, but beyond that, only the dark and endless desert. I surely stand out. There is something unmistakably foreign about me here. I'm not armed, for one. But perhaps, in spite of my shawl and long beard, I just look like a backpacker trying to fit in. Then again, it's unlikely they've ever seen a backpacker; they might think I'm a CIA agent.

I start to feel sick again halfway through the night. Perhaps I haven't fully recovered. By the time we make our first stop, my belly is bubbling painfully. Being sick in a comfortable guesthouse is bad enough, in a cramped bus in the desert something else entirely. There's nothing at the stop, just a little shack from which tea is sold. I wander out into the desert to shit.

Feeling moderately relieved, but still pretty awful, I return to the area where the bus has parked by the tea stall and find myself face to face with the only person who stands out as much in this crowd as I do—he is calm and dignified, his beard trimmed more neatly than the other men, and wears the long, dark robes of a Shia cleric.

"Hello," he says warmly. "Where are you from?" And we begin to talk. I tell him that I am American; he tells me that he is not only a cleric—he is also a smuggler. He kindly advises me about how to navigate the border.

We continue to the border, through the desert, through the night. When we finally reach the border town, it's still dark. I'm left holding my bag and my belly in the darkness.

Although it's too dark to see much, we appear to be in a small village. I wander out into the desert to shit, and when I return, hear a voice, speaking to me in English. "The border doesn't open for another two hours," he says. It is my cleric/smuggler friend. "Come, drink tea." He leads me to a little shack where a group of men sit around a small fire. He says something I can't comprehend, and they give me some tea.

In time, they all wander off, and so do I. Again, I go off into the desert to shit—will this ever end?—and return to the now-empty village. I find some burlap sacks and lie back on them looking up into the heavens. The stars become my own eyes, exploding into my consciousness. The infinite depths of space, stars from millions of years ago, stars that could now be gone and exploding into oblivion. Orion's cartwheels. The Pleiades "Glitter[ing] like a swarm of fire-flies tangled in a silver braid."

I remember my own terror and amazement at the infiniteness of space as a child. I loved to watch the stars, and they scared the shit out of me. I couldn't fathom the depth of space, couldn't imagine my own place in the infinite cosmos.

At that moment, I remember it is Christmas. Having spent the last months focused on Islam—and being no more of a Christian than anything else anyway—I haven't thought much about Christmas until that moment.

Christmas, you see, is rather low-key in the tribal areas of western Pakistan.

But the stars can teach me something deeper about Christmas than anything I've ever heard from any pulpit as a child. The stars—the brightest things in the cosmos—can teach me something about the darkness. The stars, as far from me as anything I will ever see, can teach me something about intimacy. I am in the desert, in my own mind and in the world, alone and cold and sick. This is what the authors of the Christmas story knew: the light comes in the darkest of times; god is born in the humblest of places. I've come here from places that are always well-lit—so much so that we cannot even see the stars at night. This has made us fear the darkness, shun it, turn not only from the dark places in the world but also from the dark places in us. Imagine the poems that would never have been written if we were never able to see the stars.

Only in the dark can we see the stars.

It is as if I've now crossed through the hourglass of the great Asian continent. Into Iran, from East to West. The border is as easy as my cleric/smuggler friend promised—he waves to me happily as we part ways on the other side.

I find a bus to Bam, the closest place of consequence in the area. The driver scrawls words in marker on my bag in Farsi—I'll never find out what it says. The bus is more comfortable than the one on the Pakistani side. Everything here will be—it's cleaner, quieter, more urbane and orderly. But I am still uncomfortable, still sick.

After a short time, the bus abruptly stops. A policeman enters. He scans the bus and quickly notices me. After saying something in Farsi I don't understand, he switches to English. "Passport?" I hand it over. He looks at it. Then me. "You are an *American*?" He's more surprised than hostile. I turn my head to the side, nodding in the way that they do in that part of the world.

The entire bus stops talking and turns to look. The policeman walks away with my passport. Everyone just stares in silence. A young guy sitting next to me says "American?" I nod again. He smiles and gives me a piece of his orange.

The policeman returns with my passport. "Welcome to Iran." He says, returning it. We are off. I am in pain, but happy not to be detained.

The bus breaks down before we reach Bam. I'm in agony. It's nighttime again, and this isn't the desert. Iran is clean and organized. I can't just take a shit on the side of the road. But my orange-bearing friend helps me out. He hitches me a ride straight to a hotel in Bam and arranges the fee for me. I awake the next morning feeling completely better—no more diarrhea, only memories of the stars.

Bam is quiet and small, known for its wonderful dates and its ruins. There is essentially a second city, the ruins of an ancient citadel town abandoned hundreds of years ago. I am left alone to wander the ruins for hours. I imagine what it would be like to be a future explorer, a future excavator, playing and picking through the ruins of my own civilization. A couple of years later, the ruins will be ruined again, destroyed in an earthquake.

15. THE WANDERING ARAMEAN

2001

> "My father was a wandering Aramean..."
> —DEUTERONOMY 26:5

It seems now that I am traveling from ruins to ruins, from Bam to Petra, and from some other, deeper ruin in my own heart, ancient cave paintings etched on my soul. These are memories, alive in me somehow, but also there is something in me that has fallen apart, something I need desperately to put back together. But I do not know how, only how to walk among the ruins, to walk past the ruins, from one collapsed civilization, one collapsed heart, to the next.

The thing about ruins is that we spend our time climbing over the things that are left, but the real thing about it is what used to be there, the hole in the world that we fill with the imagination, entire lives, as rich and complex as our own, that no longer exist, absences shaped like things we can only dream of. We could spend a lifetime trying to fill the absences. But it can never be done.

I arrive in Jordan at midday, exhausted from my overnight flight, to the stares of the border security who surely suspect CIA or some other connection. But they let me pass. I find a cheap hotel on a narrow street. The room has a television and I turn it on. It's the 1986 World Cup, Argentina v. England. *The Hand of God*. Maradona mocks the English, first with his trickery, then with his brilliance, to send Argentina into the semifinals. I go out for some bread and hummus, then return to pass out.

I've come to Jordan after passing through Yazd, an empty place of mud buildings and the ancient home of the Zoroastrian Fire Temple, monotheists before Islam, bringers of dualistic apocalypticism to the Israelites, whom they treated with respect after the Babylonian captivity. The Zoroastrians were particularly known for their dualism, the division of the world into absolutes of good and evil, and saw the cosmos as headed toward their inevitable confrontation and reconciliation. Their fires still burn, even if there are barely any of them left. But their ideas seem to live on, in an even more extreme and destructive ways. What is the so-called clash of civilizations but a projection onto the world of such dualism, such apocalyptic thinking? There, I met an English speaker at an internet café who's thrilled to meet an American. He told me how he wants to come to America to attend Harvard. He wants to talk about American football—even I, having grown up watching it, couldn't disagree that it's crazy and violent. He suggests that perhaps he's queer. I wonder what it's like to be queer in Iran, but don't ask.

I moved on to Isfahan, with its bridges and teahouses, its square and its mosque. Finally, I left for Tehran, with its billboards, helpfully translated into English, decrying the Great Satan, America. In spite of the rhetoric, all the Iranians I met seemed to want to know more about America, seemed tired of their theocratic government. I had to fly around Iraq. It's a no-fly zone, regularly bombed by my government. So I took a late night flight, into the morning, through the glittering oil-money mall of an airport in Bahrain, to Amman.

Amman is a city as quiet as the desert. Ruins are scattered about the city, but they are simply places to congregate—public, communal spaces, not tourist sites. The next day, I wander into a Roman amphitheater. A young man approaches. He is thin and tall, clean shaven, and carries himself in a dignified but relaxed manner. He introduces himself and explains that he is a student. His English is flawless.

I tell him my name and say I'm from America, that my journey will eventually take me to Israel. He smiles. "We call Israel the 51st state."

"I am a refugee," he explains. "My family is originally from Palestine. But I have lived most of my life in Jordan, except for the time I was studying in Germany. Now, I have an education, credentials, but I am stateless, without the rights of citizenship."

"What is the solution?" I ask. "What would you do to solve this problem, this conflict?"

"For us," he says, "It is simple. We don't care about religion. Some of us are Christian, some are Muslim. And I have no problem with Jews. I've known many Jews. For us, the solution is democracy: We want a single state, encompassing Gaza, Israel, and the West Bank, with equal rights for all."

I know this is a political impossibility, as I am sure he does. But I can't disagree.

I think of Ariel Sharon's visit to al-Aqsa Mosque and the uprising it sparked. The Second *Intifada*. As I travel ever to the west, I know I am walking into a tense and violent situation. But I have no other way to walk.

From Amman, I travel south to the ruins of Petra, a city carved into cliffs. The uprising has left such sites completely without the Western tourists who normally flood them. I stay in the cheapest hotel, the farthest from the site. I walk past them all, grander and grander, as I walk to Petra, and don't see a soul except for a Bedouin or two selling trinkets or tea. It is a city carved into rock and cliff. In other words, it is a place that was revealed rather than made, defined more by its absences than its presence. I feel at home there. The site itself is empty, a great playground for me to imagine civilizations past or, perhaps, just as the death of a parent or grandparent invites reflection on one's own mortality, I again imagine the destruction of my own civilization, its ruins a future playground for another wanderer. I cross the vast and empty desert of Wadi Rum, where I spend my days wandering across sand dunes, nights in a tent in contemplation of the stars. In Egypt I dive into coral reefs, an explosion of color, calm and shallow at first, before I reach the edge. It's an abyss, unimaginably deep. It's almost terrifying, like leaping off the edge of a cliff. But leaping into the abyss is rewarded: the colors of life are found in the depths, like the autumn colors in the Berkshires, like Altamira. Perhaps God isn't on the top of the mountain, but under the sea, the depths again. Nonetheless, I climb to the top of Mt Sinai on my way to Cairo, before turning back north, to Israel.

When I arrive at the Rafah border, we're searched first on the Egyptian side. They did not care to search me at all entering Egypt, but seem anxious here—there is international pressure for them to keep this border, into Gaza, safe. I'm allowed through and sent to an open air waiting area. A young and pretty Palestinian woman smiles flirtatiously with me. We wait some more, for hours. I ask someone what we are waiting for. The bus, I am told. Finally, it arrives. We all get in. We move ahead maybe one hundred feet, then stop.

"Why are we stopped?" I ask an older Palestinian man.

"We are here," he says. "We can get off."

"Why didn't we just walk?" I say.

"They just want to make us wait," he answers with a shrug. "Just to… just to… just to fuck with us."

I nod and exit the bus.

We are now separated according to nationality. Palestinians in one line; EU, USA, and Israel passport holders in the other. There are many more Palestinians, and no Israelis. I am the only American in a line with perhaps five or six Europeans.

While the Palestinians wait—they are perpetually waiting in this world, always in some sort of security line—our line moves relatively quickly. Until it's my turn. Seeing the array of Middle Eastern stamps on my passport, I'm taken into a separate room where I'm searched and interrogated for an hour. The Israeli security forces take themselves very seriously, with reflective sunglasses and grim expressions. Finally, seeing no reason to deny my entry, I'm allowed to pass.

Those of us heading into Israel proper are taken to a military vehicle by a young soldier. "It's just that… we've had some… *problems*," he explains apologetically as he directs us into the back of the armored vehicle. I watch out through the narrow slits as we ride on smooth Israeli roads bordered by barbed wire fences, beyond which are ragged settlements amid decaying infrastructure and a parched, barren landscape.

Finally, we reach Israel. I ride on a bus now, a clean and comfortable coach bus. The view through these windows is not only wider than the narrow slits of the military vehicle: the desert here has been made green; the stores filled with expensive Western goods. Young Israeli soldiers chat away on their cell phones—not yet a common site in America. One soldier giggles—she looks to be about 18—when she drops her Tavor Assault Rifle.

I am staying at a youth hostel in the Old City in Jerusalem. I'm told that this is a place normally packed with foreign backpackers, but it's quiet now. Soldiers nervously stand at every major entry point to the Old City. Non-Muslims aren't allowed to enter al-Aqsa, but I can see its famous Golden Dome from the roof of the hostel.

In my nearly empty hostel there is Sergei, a Russian Stalinist who has paid someone off in Russia to get a visa to live in Israel. He isn't Jewish. He paints portraits of Stalin and other heroes of the fallen Soviet empire. When I tell him I'm from Chicago, he asks how many murders we had there last year, and scoffs at the low body count. "And in Russia," he brags, "ours are all by stabbing."

There is Judah, an African American who's working at the hostel to pay for his stay. He wears a long, quasi-Biblical robe and tells me he's there on a spiritual search.

Simon and Mike are Americans. Simon is a young Jew, only 18, who's been sent to Israel to work on a Kibbutz after being sent to "Marijuana Anonymous" back home for smoking too much weed. He's a nice kid, but a little naïve, a fervent Zionist. Mike is a reporter for a liberal publication I don't know. He takes us to refugee camps and for beers, trying consistently, if fruitlessly, to get Simon to see the injustice of the Israeli treatment of Palestinians.

After a few days in Jerusalem, I develop a toothache. I find a place in the Armenian Quarter where an old guy will fix it for cheap. But I don't realize until he's hit my tooth that he isn't going to use Novocaine. The pain is excruciating, but temporary, and he seems to have fixed the problem.

I leave the Old City to find a smoothie bar, not wanting to chew yet with my recently-repaired tooth. I arrive just as the rain starts, first slow, then torrential. "Tibet!" says the guy running the smoothie shop pointing to my hate, which says "Tibet" on it. "Have you been to Dharamsala?"

I tell him that I haven't, that I got the hat in Tibet.

"That's cool... Free Tibet!" he says with a smile. "I went to India, to Dharamsala, spent some time there after I left the army."

I nod and order a smoothie. My tooth still hurts, but it's not so bad. The rain continues.

"It's really pouring out there, huh?" he goes on. His expression changes. "Well, we can use it. We give all our water to the fucking Arabs."

I pay for my smoothie and leave to drink it in the rain.

Jerusalem is tense. I can feel this tension with every step, in every interaction. Its ancient walls can barely contain the tension. The air is heavy with thousands of years of conflict, someone tells me. This is true. But this feels too easy, a copout. The tension is new, too. It is born of the geopolitics of today, of the irreconcilability of Europe's guilt over the holocaust and Israel's treatment of the Palestinians. It isn't as simple as another European colonial project. It isn't that. But it's also a devil's bargain: To become a nation state requires so many things that cannot possibly be accounted for in the story of a people's suffering. It requires the purchase of weapons; it even, in this case, requires the Jewish state to make an alliance with fundamentalist Christians on the other side of the globe who hope to bring about the End Times in which the Jews themselves will not be saved.

I am ready for some quiet, some space—Jerusalem is packed and cramped with stone walls and absurd contradictions. I head north, to the Galilee, stopping in Safed. This is the place where Lurianic Kabbalah flowered, where Jews who'd been expelled from Spain had created a community in which they believed that their work was to heal a broken world— repairing the divine vessels that had shattered in creation. For them the work of healing the self—*tikkun nefesh*—was no different from healing the world—*tikkun olam*. I think maybe I will find more sense among the Jewish mystics than I can contemplating the Jewish nation state. What I do find is a lovely hilltop town, an artist colony. The mosques and homes of displaced Palestinians have been taken over and to be used by Israeli artists.

I do find serenity in the Galilee. It's warmer and sunnier than Jerusalem. Riding a bike around the Sea of Galilee, I meet an American Jew who has deeply conflicted feelings about Israel. We talk about this and other things, passing monuments to the works of Jesus, that Jew from long ago who lived in an occupied Palestine.

Indeed, Jesus lived in a world in which his people were under siege. Politically, they faced global powers—the Romans—that they could not hope to overcome. Economically, they were pushed to the brink, into destitution and even slavery. Culturally they were faced with a cosmopolitan Hellenistic worldview that nullified their old ways of making meaning—the story of their people that centered on the Jewish Temple. Having lost their traditional means of production, they were often forced to sell their labor; having lost their traditional means of making meaning, they were often forced to sell their souls.

Some of the Israelites—the Zealots—fought back. But they never had a chance. Jesus, the peasant from Galilee, offered another option. If we can simply change our perspective, we can usher in the apocalypse, a radical re-imagining of our place in the world. It was easy to sell this to his contemporaries;

they could see the end of things all around. But what he meant was neither an acceptance of Roman power nor a military rebellion. Rather, he preached a transformation of our selves and a reimagining of what salvation means. The Temple would no longer be on the mountaintop, but in the human heart. If only we have ears to hear, and eyes to see.

The stories passed down from generation to generation in the Levant will eventually be compiled into a book. The Jewish people, as they come to be known, will call this book holy. The book, the stories themselves, will replace the temple. Europeans will eventually get their hands on this book, and they will call it holy, too. Even the colonizers will carry the book. They tell the stories through a different lens, a different worldview, and remake them.

Eventually, the enslaved people of what will be called, absurdly, the "new world" will hear the stories, including those that are called the "Old Testament." In spite of the fact that the stories are given to them by the enslavers, they will see something that the enslavers could not: that these were stories about a people seeking collective liberation, a people becoming a people in their shared pursuit of freedom. They would understand better than anyone that their work in this world was to care for the stranger in hard times, to make the stranger into kin. This was the miracle of the Bible, the stories from the Holy Land.

I fly from Tel Aviv to Napoli, the chaotic and beautiful city of my ancestors. From there, I find Sergio in Ischia. He gives me a bike and I ride each day around the island. It's midwinter, and without the tourists the island feels empty. In the evenings I meet up with Sergio. On my last night, he brings me to a family celebration. I eat and drink, understanding little of what is said. An old woman sits on my lap.

I return to Napoli to wander the streets, streets that are themselves works of art, twisted and labyrinthine, narrow and rutted. These streets have texture, unlike the Euclidian grid of the Chicago I've left. I can hear the texture in the dialect, taste it and smell it in the Vesuvian soil of tomatoes and flowers sold at the market. This is a Mediterranean city—a city in the middle of the world, intersections of peoples and languages and cultures. All of these things make it rich and deep. But now, in a shallow world, it is poor, scorned by the north, its shaded, textured people called "Arabs". When the football club travels to Milan, the northerners sing songs about how dirty the southerners are, mocking them for their cholera outbreaks and volcanic eruptions.

When my ancestors left, just like the people I encountered in Zimbabwe and Pakistan and Vietnam, it was the textured world, the world they loved and knew, the place where their ancestors' bodies were buried in the earth and eaten every day in their bread, where their ancestors songs were sung each day in the dialect—they traded all this to participate in the capitalist world, a world that lacked the dimension not only of depth but also of time: emigration required them to forget their participation in the timeless. They had to forget who they were and all they'd left. So my own ancestors forgot it all, and left behind their depth and their memories, the dirty streets of Napoli for the wealth and promise of New Jersey.

I take the train up the coast to Rome. Again, the city is emptied of tourists—and all the more beautiful for it. I wander into churches and drink wine in the piazzas. And then I move on again, stopping in Florence, its echoes of Dante, and Venice, its twisted streets a work of poetry in itself. Venice is cold and misty. And sinking—like New Orleans, it is being swallowed by the sea, reduced to a mere museum.

I ride on a train from Venice to Paris in a sleeper car with two couples, each sleeping across from one another. The bed across from me is empty.

It is here that the end begins.

Here, in gray, gay, lonely Paris, I sense, for the first time, that my journey is ending. I am neither happy nor sad. I am nothing. Empty. For this journey is, in many ways, an emptying.

I feel so far away from anything and everything.

I have seen so many places, been so many things. I have crossed borders into the depths of my own heart that I did not know existed. I have crossed mountains, deserts and jungles. I have crossed borders so seldom crossed. I walk through these cold, broad streets wearily—my feet hurting from the months of walking; my tooth aching from time to time; I am thin and bald; there is a scar over my right eye—but I feel as though I can keep moving forever. I realize that as difficult as traveling can be, it can be more difficult to stop.

I have been everything in the eyes of those I've encountered: strange and exotic; a crook and a cheat; annoying and selfish and suspicious. I have been grotesque. I am all that I fear and abhor on the faces of those I have encountered.

And now I begin my descent from the thin air and barren ground of the stark mountaintop. I am transported, in my mind, to Mt. Sinai, looking across the desert, seeing nothing but nothingness, rock upon dry, barren rock. I am there. Here in the café and at the bread shop, listening to jazz and hip hop, I am atop the lonely mountain. I *am* the mountain—barren and dry and empty. I scarcely remember the landscape to which I will return, don't know if it will still feel like home. And now I am falling into the depths, looking for a home that is not a place but a feeling.

I will soon return to the place—America, Chicago—whence I came. This journey—like all journeys—will be a circle, beginning and ending at the same point, so different and so much the same.

Before they came across the sea to America they had been tailors and coalminers.

The Welsh are from a little village where the River Teifi meets the sea. St. Dogmaels is its name. It is famous for the ruins of St. Dogmaels abbey. Appropriately, somehow, these ancestors come from a village that once was a spiritual center and from a country known for its poets, for the patriarch of the American family will become a preacher.

Little is known about the genesis of his calling or about the nature of his ordination. He seems to have been self-educated, self-ordained. What's more, he, like so many other young men, will sail across the sea to remake himself: it is an autopoetic voyage; he is not merely a poet—a maker of worlds—but a self-maker. He is self-named. But just as his journey across the sea provides the possibility of newness, it also allows for a clearer remembrance of the old. He names himself Teifion. And Teifion Richards is brought to America, to the coal mines of Scranton, PA, to preach in Welsh, the language of the old country.

He marries into American Puritanism but never really fits in. His wife, my great grandmother, tries to push him toward temperance, but this is never really his scene. Teifion is a man of the people, as comfortable in the speak-easy as in the pulpit. He has been brought to Scranton to preach to coalminers, not aristocrats.

His son, my grandfather, is inspired by this egalitarian ethic and goes to college, then seminary, to study in the tradition of the social gospel, to preach among the felons and the homeless.

The Italians aren't even really Italian. Only a few decades since the formation of the Italian state, they surely consider themselves Neapolitan first, Italian second. Like the Welsh, they are a part of a nation state from which they are a people apart, speaking perhaps some of the language, but not as well as their mother tongue. Unlike the Welsh, however, they are urban, eking out a living as tailors in the concrete jungle that is Naples; and unlike the Welsh, they live among ruins of grand old civilizations, not of marginal settlements.

Perhaps because they've been outsiders in Italy, they work to become insiders in America. They come through Ellis Island like millions of other Italians, reviled for their brown skin and Catholicism, settling in Newark. They work hard and raise their children to be Americans, giving them names like Betty and Rose. Amazingly, they send all six off to college. My mother was born an American, fully immersed in the American dream, raised in suburban 1950s New Jersey—her mother has left Newark behind along with Catholicism and dialect, just as her grandparents have left Naples—to work hard for its own joyless sake.

The preacher takes his first son to his work with him, where he ministers to the men at the bottom: drunks and homeless, criminals and outcasts. The preacher instills in the son a sense of justice, the prophetic tradition of the social gospel. He advocates the civil rights movement, even taking his family for a semester to Virginia Union, a Black college. But my father is a son of the fifties, too, and never quite takes part in the counter-culture of the sixties. He goes off to college, then Vietnam. He leaves parts of himself in the war—as his son, I know this only because all young men who go off to war do so, not because he ever tells me—and brings things back with him that become a part of the man I know. I know neither the boy before the war nor how to distinguish the parts of the man, my father, which are brought home from the war, like mistaken luggage, any better than I knew the preacher Teifion. He marries my mother when he comes home, goes to law school, and goes to work.

My mother works, too: her work is a son, then another. She is a teacher. Whereas the Welsh made meaning through words like poets and preachers do, the Italians go from tailors to teachers. All of them teach: uncles and aunts; grandmothers and grandfathers. She teaches me, and then my brother. There are many things we never learn, like fixing things and sharing feelings, but she gives us two great gifts: we will know how to care for those we love and we will know how to think.

While they brought a few memories, and of course many genetic markers that I carry on my body, I can only ponder the traumas they've passed on, like the color of my eyes and the shape of my nose. I wonder, when there are demons in me that seem not to have any cause, if they've come from my dark and unknown past.

If I could ask the ancestors, or the ancestors of my children who trod paths far different from my own, how they survived, how I got here in spite of it all—the suffering, the absolute impossibility of our existence—I think they would say this: The secret of life is that family is made rather than given, a verb as much as it is a noun. They discovered that they could take despair and loneliness and make family, something like the alchemical process that turned bacteria into flourished ecosystems of care and, eventually, love.

I make my way, finally, to Wales, where I find a youth hostel in the coastal town of Fishguard. I rent a bike and ride through the countryside each day. I visit St. Dogmaels and see the little house where my great grandfather was born. I ride to St. David's, pierced by the wind, frozen, with only my Pakistani shawl to keep me warm.

I peer out over the cliffs into the western sea. The wind is intense here, bringing together the texture of air, land, sea. There really is no boundary between land and sea—the wind carries with it the salty taste of the ocean, of loneliness and connection. I have nearly completed the circle. But what does it mean? Can I see now that the Earth is a circle? Can I now see the impossibility of running away? Just as when I returned from Africa, I will fly in a sterile, soulless, atemporal machine across the ocean, reaching out for the stars. I will wonder, years later, if I ever made it back, wonder if, rather than returning to Chicago I plunged into the sea. Wonder if everything else was my encounter with the depths. The real journey.

PART III
PARADISO

All'altra fantasia qui manco possa;
Ma gia volgeva il mio disiro e il velle,
Si come rota ch'egualmente e mossa,
L'amor che move il sole e l'altre stelle.

—DANTE, *PARADISO*, CANTO XXXIII, 142-145

16. INSANITY
2001

Having traveled around the world, having experienced that if you walk long enough you always arrive back at your starting point, I can see clearly that the way we are living is crazy. I have seen the absolute poverty, heard the coughing, the choking on the dirty air, felt the gentle movement of a spherical and finite planet. We are running out of water and air and space. We are killing ourselves.

The world has gone mad. And I suppose that I am the craziest of them all, thinking I could escape myself, escape this little island planet as it swims through the galaxy. I hear news of madness's manifestation from home, from the place I've run from. My brother has been diagnosed with clinical depression, Denise with schizophrenia.

While the masses of Africa and Asia suffer, seeking dwindling treasures on an island planet that has only so much, there is another kind of suffering, of madness, that I can now see more clearly since I've been around the world. The world, the real world, is filled with suffering, with blood and dirt. But it also has beauty. It is something to taste—it has texture, depth, unlike the two-dimensional mall, the screen world hell to which we've all been damned. Somehow, I have to remember how to taste the world, to remember its texture, its depth. Staring at our screens, we've all become impossibly wealthy and comfortable and lonely.

While some of us descend into madness, most find a way to cope with the cycle of shame and denial that captivates us. In a world filled with individual addicts, there is also a collective addiction. Dopamine is everywhere: bottles, bags, and screens. It makes a heavy world feel a little lighter. But it makes us weaker, too. And what if the world itself becomes the addict? What if the world has become too weak to hold our heavy hearts?

The paradox of polycrisis is this: We must figure out how to fall in love with the world as a whole, its immensity, its complexity, to experience its depth and its texture. But none of these things make any sense without experiencing an intimacy with the particular. To mourn for the children of the world requires us to know what it means to love a child; to fall in love with the world requires us to know what it means to fall in love with an individual. To begin to heal the world requires us to begin to confront our own wounds. And this is so much harder. For the world's wounds can seem far away, an abstraction. And falling in love with an idea, an abstraction, can be so much easier than the messy prospect of falling in love with a single soul. These two things—healing and loving—are entangled. For it is when we fall in love that all our wounds become exposed.

9-11 comes to me on the radio—I have no television at the time. When it becomes apparent what is happening, I ride my bike over to my friend Nick's house. We watch silently.

Then, as days and weeks and months pass, everything changes. One war, then another. All around me is the madness of patriotism. There is a world on fire, a world desperately needing to be one world—if nothing else, I now know this—but it is a world that cannot help but be at war with itself. The places I've passed through are under siege. The Taliban—the men with rifles who rode on buses and pickups through Quetta, perhaps—are the enemy. Or, perhaps, it is Islam itself. The clash of civilizations, for me, seems more like a war between fundamentalisms.

Without a flag to wave, I feel alone in the vast world, knowing just how big and how small our world has become.

Antonio and I have never lost track of one another. He has traveled to England, twice—an immeasurably long journey given his background and resources. In his travels, he has fallen in love with Chelsea Football Club.

I now support the clubs of my ancestors—Napoli and Swansea—who are wallowing in the lower divisions of Italy and England, as well as Barcelona. Barca, as they are known, will become the great club of the early 21st century. I love them for their style. They play what Pele called "the beautiful game"—soccer that is as much art as sport. Winning is secondary; it is expression that counts. Chelsea, for those who appreciate the beautiful game, is an abomination, a win-at-all-costs club, a club run by Russian oil money rather than the supporters.

But Antonio loves them. And there is something of an accusation in this love. He loves them for their lack of style, lack of history. Loves their struggle. He believes Barcelona to be a bourgeois indulgence. For Antonio—and he is not alone in this—his deepest, most heartfelt identity—even as a Black man—is completely enmeshed in his notions of class. He despises the Black middle class, mocks white liberals. He prefers the Chelsea supporters and their working-class racism.

The whole world begins to watch football now, even Americans. It is no longer a thing for world travelers to indulge in. No longer my secret. Antonio and I argue about this and other things, even as we see ourselves as something more than the average American soccer fan. We argue the most, it seems, with those with whom we most often agree.

How is it that we can be friends, Antonio and me? I can only come up with one answer: There is an outsiderness to us. This is why he found me in the eighth grade; why I even went to East High; why Sue found me and pulled me out of the University of Chicago; why I couldn't find a place on the basketball team; why I always looked for god and never joined a church; why I always, every chance I got, wandered; why I even could bear the absolute loneliness of the road.

And still, even as I forced myself apart, the thing I desired most was something—a womb, a family, a community—to be inside.

17. SUE: "WHY?"

"Why, Sue?" I ask. She knows what I mean, even though I don't explain it. It needs no explanation.

I have just told her that I am leaving. This time, perhaps, for good. She has always been supportive of my wandering, even if it is so far from her own path. When I tell her, she only holds her dog and looks out across her yard, to the garden that she has described as her salvation. Gardens, children, books. These are her gods.

She has spent most of her life on the south side of Chicago, even if remnants of a New England accent linger on her tongue. She has seldom traveled. There were years when she seldom even took a day off. Even Christmas.

I am there to talk about the children and about the center. These things are her life. Inseparable from who she is. I tell her about what's going on with the Jones family, the Hughes family, the Freemans. She nods. David Jones is contemplating his next steps, thinking of college, I tell her.

It is summer now. Sue is hot and uncomfortable. More than once, she has told me that she prefers the winter. This is partly due to the fact that she sweats in the heat, but also because Chicago's summers bring guns and death. I know this and don't have to ask why.

But when I tell her about my plans to leave, she tells me how she decided to stay, how she never felt the urge to wander off. Never even to pause to celebrate a holiday. This is when I ask her.

Why?

"We all have to choose what to do with our lives," she says, "to do something good with the little time we have."

There is a pause, as always, as she seems to sniff the air and listen for squirrels like her dogs.

"So, what is David Jones doing?" she asks. I begin to tell her that I've already told her that. Then I stop, realizing that this is the stuff of the conversations we have with the people we love. We listen to the same stories. Answer the same questions. We try to remember each other, not the details.

I begin to tell her again as the late summer air, thick with Lake Michigan and Chicago grime, begins to cool. She will ask and re-ask about the children and their families. I wonder what this means.

18. BRAZIL
2003

I HAVE ONE MORE CONTINENT, AND I AM RUNNING OUT OF TIME. I am twenty-nine years old. I have things to figure out. I can see that this life—a couple of years at Sue and a year away—can't last forever. I have ideas to explore, stories to tell. But I have more to see. And I want to see the place where Africa flourished in what they called "the new world".

I've come to Brazil for further adventure, to visit a continent I've not yet seen. I have been thinking that maybe I'll do something different now—leave Chicago, fall in love again, go to school. I don't know.

What is it that I might do with this blink-of-an-eye life? This is what I have come to Brazil to ask. This is perhaps all I've ever been looking for: When I find the ocean or the nighttime sky, I am facing immensity, and my own smallness. We are born and, in a flash of lightning, we have become old and wonder where our youth went. Our children grow old. We die. There is nothing we can do to make it last—a life that lasts for fifty years or a hundred is still nothing in the cosmos. And so there are a thousand philosophies that tell us how it lasts, where the self, a something that endures beyond the flesh, can last. But what if it doesn't? Or even if it does, what does a soul consist of after a soulless life? I have to figure out how to be soulful, even if just for a blink of an eye. I have to remember the texture of the world, to taste it, to encounter its depth, and mine. My eternity depends on it.

I meet up with Becky in Rio, where I've found a dingy motel near the beach. She has been my foil and friend before it all, before I even left for Africa, before I traveled around the world. She is brilliant and annoying. She loves me and despises me. I am ready to travel alone and she is looking for companionship. For me, she is something like a memory, and a confrontation with my own fetishization of the lonely road. It is never going to work.

From the moment we meet up in Rio, Becky irritates me. She is a maddening person. One of the smartest I've known. And well-read. Moreover, she has a feel for ideas, for literature. We should be great friends. But the truth is that it is hard for us to be in the same room together. I met her during the time I lived on the mountain, preparing for my work in Zimbabwe. She was headed to Angola. A small woman with big opinions—skinny but pretty in an androgynous sort of way—she paid almost no attention to the staff running the training, choosing instead to chain smoke hand-rolled cigarettes and read novels. She likes men but hates the fact that she does; she is attracted to me and particularly hates this fact.

We carry this tension around with us, like old letters in a shoebox, until a confluence of events brings us to Rio. I have various reasons for travel, none of which involve Becky.

Rio is a mosaic of color, tropical forests and shimmering beaches, rocky mountains, like Corcovado, interspersed among its colonial buildings, people of every shade, rhythms of Africa, but reimagined. It is an entire world to explore. For an American, coming from a dualistic, Protestant, *cold* world of the north, one is struck most at the blurred lines of

Catholic, African Brazil, a taste of which I got years before in New Orleans.

Maybe I've come to Brazil to ask myself a simple question: is it possible for me to find my way home? *Home*. I've been taught that home was a place, static. But how is this even possible when you've wandered so much, when you've come to see that the place you left, like the flowing river, is never the same. Time insinuates itself; change becomes apparent. In Brazil, I remember the lessons of those who came here by force, torn away from Africa. It turns out that these things that we thought were static can be *made*. Afro-Brazilians will make family out of those who land next to them, make a world out of their imagination, make home out of the place in which they find themselves. Traumatic as the Middle Passage was, it showed them that home was found in relationship as much as place. And this is the stuff with which the world is made.

Becky has a different expectation than I for the trip, and we constantly quarrel. She wants a regular companion and is annoyed that I want to go off on my own. Moreover, it becomes clear that she also wants *protection*. "I'm blonde!" she cries. "I can't just go wandering around on my own here!"

There is a graffito across the street from where we are staying: YANKEE GO HOME!

Nonetheless, we persist in Rio. Its surf is warm, its juice bars, delicious. Its neighborhoods are varied and interesting. Although it has its share of poverty and crime, there is also enough of a middle class there that I can get out and see its variety. But Becky and I really came here to experience Bahia—on this much we can agree.

It's evening when we arrive in Salvador, and I've found a hostel in the Pelourinho area, the old, colonial center of Salvador. Its proprietor is a gorgeous woman, as are all the staff, who seem to take a liking to me. I am good with Portuguese and make an effort to talk to them. There is some level of mutual attraction between a staff member and me, annoying her boyfriend who comes by periodically. Bahian breakfast is a work of art. A vast table filled with every kind of tropical fruit imaginable. The staff pays less attention to Becky, who is struggling with Portuguese. I love the place. Becky is less impressed and wants to leave.

We do agree that Salvador is not exactly what we are looking for—even for me, in spite of my happiness with the hostel. The old city *looks* beautiful. Throughout the day, groups like *Filhos di Gandhi* march through town, drumming. It is an African place, with African rhythms. But it's also touristy. There are tourist police guarding its edges, keeping the locals away. For beyond the old city are the *favelas*, poverty and violence. In spite of the beauty, in spite of the African drums, there is a sterility to the Pelourinho. Or maybe there is something else; it is, after all, the name not of the historic center of the town; it is the name for the whipping post where slaves were punished, publicly, brutally.

This is the tension that Brazil, and Bahia in particular, carries. It is a place of blurred lines, of less rigid racial categories than in North America or other more dualistic, Protestant places. It is possible, regardless of one's shade, to be Brazilian, first and foremost. Unlike the United States, there is no "one drop rule" that has rendered anyone with any amount of African ancestry to be wholly Black, wholly *other*. But while these nuances are perhaps preferable—something North Americans could learn from—they do not make Brazil a racial paradise. Racism persists.

I am finally able to see more of Salvador at the *Festa do Bonfim*, a celebration of the Afro-Brazilian religion, brought through the Middle Passage, known here as *Candomble—Santeria* in Spanish countries, *Vodoun* in French ones. The Africans, forbidden to worship their own gods, saw something that the Europeans could not: The saints were really just polytheistic gods in disguise. When Christianity came to Europe, and the worship of local gods was forbidden, some of those gods became saints. So when the Africans were stolen away to the Americas, they realized that the only way to keep their religion alive was to hide it—perhaps as Europeans had, millennia ago—in the gods of their oppressors. So Catholic saints come to be associated with Yoruba *Orishas*.

I buy white linen and join the thousands of other singing, beer drinking revelers, through the streets of Salvador, to the Basilica of *Nosso Senhor do Bonfim*. The procession is led by women, Yoruba priestesses. The Catholic priests are followers here. When they arrive at the church, they wash the steps, singing Yoruba songs, remembered after so many generations, from Africa.

I take excursions out of Salvador, first to Cachoeira, the home of the Maes da Boa Morte, African priestesses devoted to the "good death." They remind us that everything, including us, dies. Such a teaching is an anathema in American religion, where, in any pulpit—New Age, Fundamentalist, Capitalist—one often hears the gospel of prosperity. Of abundance. We can have it all, live longer, live painlessly. The descendants of slaves who choose to remember the Middle Passage can also remember that there are limits to what we can have, limits to how long we have.

Cachoeira is quiet, with little nightlife or really anything to do. But there is a gentle river, and somewhere a waterfall after which it is named. It has a good color to it, and a spaciousness that I could never find in Salvador or Rio, with their crowded and narrow streets. Cachoeira is yellow buildings, surrounded by lush green. Dotted with black shrines to the Orishas.

From there I meet with Becky in Lencois. It's a New Agey kind of a place, pleasant but with some of the taste of those backpacker spots I've always turned my nose up at. I am doing this with Becky, too, who feels more comfortable in Lencois and has begun to think of me as a backpacking snob and who isn't willing enough to party. She thinks I'm too serious; I think she's too comfortable with her American privilege. We bicker and part for good. I take treks alone in the jungle, leaping off of cliffs in waterfall-fed pools, sliding down natural waterslides.

I return to Salvador. I don't really want to be there even though I'm back at my favorite youth hostel. I feel stuck in the historical center, surrounded by tourists and tourist police. I'm alone now, and need to be more alone. I realize that I might not have such a chance again. I am longing for something, something in me that is painful, something like a birth, or a good death. I travel north, looking for a lonely beach.

19. *SITIO DO CONDE*
2003

FIVE YEARS AFTER I LEFT MOZAMBIQUE, I FIND MYSELF IN ANOTHER PORTUGUESE-SPEAKING BEACH. Sitio do Conde is a town several hours north of Salvador. I have come there for the promise, only a short walk from town, of a vast and empty beach. The town is a tiny little place, a small hotel and a simple restaurant serving basic Brazilian fare—*feijoada* and little else. The town square is a grassy patch where the children play soccer.

Each day, I walk south from my hotel along the beach. There is an abandoned beach bar for shade and rest. I can hear the jackhammers in the distance. They are building a new road. New hotels will follow. This won't be a lonely beach for long. We are spreading out across the globe, filling in every crack, the ultimate invasive species. We are destroying the planet. What if life itself, too, is just a blink of an eye? What if, like my own life, the entire process of life on Earth was a mere flicker, a pulse of life, like an irregularity on the quantum foam, in an otherwise vast, empty, and lifeless cosmos?

Will it matter? Will my life, or the entire unfolding of life and humanity, mean any less? Will I do something different with my—and our—blink-of-an-eye?

What is your question? I hear it again, as I sit in the ruins of an old beach bar of a vast and empty beach where I've come to spend the day. I see scarcely a soul that day. No one speaks to me, just the soft rhythm of the waves. *How long will this beach remain empty?* I wonder. *How long will I?*

I am twenty-nine years old. I've wandered for most of my life. I have little money and few possessions. Perhaps, I think, the time has come to begin to answer my question.

And perhaps, now that I've been to each continent and realized that I really cannot run away, I am realizing that I never really needed or wanted to run away, that the loneliness of the road, my love of it, was something I merely convinced myself of because I was taught to fear vulnerability.

I contemplate these questions as I periodically dive into the ocean, contemplating the waves, too, each unique wave stretching out beyond the ocean, but always receding back into the whole, each something like the previous, but different; each ultimately belonging to the same ocean. It is the ocean that teaches me: I can still long for the stars even as I belong to the sea; I can still cry for the world, even as I fall in love with it.

20. MEXICO
2003

Ari moves back to Chicago while I am in Brazil. Word comes to me through a mutual friend. Then I run into her. "Give me a call," she says. I say I will. Then I don't. Then, finally, I do.

Something new has happened to me. I am ready for new things, and not just in leaving Chicago. It is as though she entered my life not merely by chance, but because my prayers to Yemaya were answered from that Bahian beach bar. I will ask no questions of this co-incidence. Indeed, for a lifetime, even as things fall apart, I will assume that this was always meant to be. We fit together, like a puzzle. But what I cannot yet see is that it is our broken parts that fit together so perfectly. I will not see it until much later, when we have cut each other open a thousand times with the sharp edges of our brokenness.

We drive down to Asheville, North Carolina together, where she's been living. I suggest, there, in the mountains, that maybe she could come to New York City with me, to live.

She says yes.

But first, I tell her, we need an adventure together.

We retrace, in reverse, the old migration route from the south, where Ari's ancestors, migrants, once traveled. We come down through Memphis, through the cotton fields of Mississippi and Arkansas. When we reach Texas, the air begins to dry, the roads straighten. Is Texas America? Have we crossed the border? It was once part of Mexico and fought a war to leave. Then, when it joined the union, it fought a war to get rid of the Comanche. Then it fought a war to leave the union, to keep its slaves. Even now, the people change before the political border does. Spanish is increasingly common.

Like all borders, the USA-Mexico border exists only in the human imagination. Men draw lines on maps and think they are real, even as they ascribe value to people and products that pass over the borders. By 2003, the border here is more or less passable depending on context: microbes and birds barely notice it; products like subsidized American corn pass freely; American guns and Mexican drugs flow consistently if illegally. But everyone only worries about the Mexican and Central American people who try to cross over, often traveling for hundreds of miles to escape poverty or violence.

The border regions on both sides are militarized. By the time we get to Corpus Christi—perhaps the most boring city I've ever been to—we have already partially entered Mexico. The food, the people, the language—it all seems more Mexican than American, whatever that might mean. Of course, it was once a part of Mexico anyway. Borders are such liars.

The scrublands of south Texas are crawling with border patrols. No one cares about us—we are heading south, not north. We pass easily from Brownsville into Matamoros, obscenely and ironically named "Moor Killer" in remembrance of another time in which Brown people from the south were shunned and removed from a land that had once been theirs.

While the culture doesn't change all that dramatically when one crosses the Rio Grande, the economy surely does. We quickly drive out of Matamoros and then pass through another, secondary border, this one perhaps even more militarized than the formal one. The border region is kept separate from the rest of Mexico, manned primarily with kids with guns and uniforms far too big for them. For me, kids with guns are scarier than mules or migrants. I stare at them blankly when they ask me questions in Spanish—I know some Spanish, but they speak fast and there doesn't seem to be an advantage to trying. Sure enough, they give up and wave me on.

We drive down the Gulf Coast, on narrow, rural roads, passing through villages, dodging falling rocks and scurrying crabs. Finally, we reach the town of La Pesca. It isn't the type of place Americans visit. It's a little beach town where middle class Mexicans might vacation. We visit the beach, but it's cloudy and windy. The weather seems to be turning. There is no internet, little news, so we don't know how to figure out the weather. We spend the night in the hotel bar, drinking beer and listening to Spanish versions of American R & B. Later, Ari sits outside our hotel room, overlooking a courtyard. A guy staying at the hotel starts to harass her—he's sloppy drunk. But he wanders off when I shoo him away. We hold each other through the night, listening to the tropical rain; the pounding, pulsing surf; and one another's heartbeats.

The weather gets worse and worse the next day. The winds pick up and it's raining harder. So we decide to leave, to head inland, to Ciudad Victoria.

Ciudad Victoria is sunny, and bigger, a small city rather than a town. There is English language news in our hotel room and CNN tells us there is a hurricane in the Gulf heading this way. It was good that we left.

We love Ciudad Victoria: its market where we can buy herbs, herbs that we'll keep for years in our cabinets, moving across the country with them; its peaceful square where couples, like us, walk arm in arm; its old church and open people, smiling at us as we take pictures. But in a few days the weather starts to turn again—the hurricane has made landfall and become a massive storm—and we take off for the north, through miserable traffic in Monterrey, across the eastern Sierra Madres and to Laredo.

The traffic there is backed up throughout the city. Thousands upon thousands, in lines extending way beyond the border area, past homes and business. What will happen, I wonder, when the farms of the global south dry up, when the seas rise, when the migrants of a shrinking, warming planet really come? Will we just build a wall around the United States? Will we trap ourselves within a prison of our own making?

What will it take for us to realize the absurdity of walls and borders between us? I think, as we pass into the United States, into the scrublands of south Texas, past the checkpoints, Ari sitting next to me, smiling, because even a world on fire can't touch you when you are young and in love, as we watch border patrol chase the Latin people through the desert, as we listen to songs, love songs, that will always be, somehow, current, because this moment will always be *always*. *"I'm coming home to you,"* sings Raphael Saadiq. *"Wear something see-through/ So I can see your heart."* I want to marry her, I realize, to have a family.

The great mystery of borders is this: We tell ourselves that they are built to keep people out, but they exist only to be crossed.

21. NEW YORK CITY
2003-2005

LOVE CAN BE AN ILLUSION, CAN BE A BAND-AID FOR OUR WOUNDS, CAN MASK OUR DESPAIR, COVER OUR SCARS. For different reasons, reasons we will not know for many years when we crash, we've each been at the brink of falling off a cliff. Perhaps our love is a leap off together—is this why they call it falling in love?—and we so desperately need to hold onto something that we hold onto each other, hold on so tight that we won't even realize we are falling until many years later when we crash into the earth, or perhaps the sea, where the thing that will die won't be us but the illusion itself.

We move to New York together. I am there to study religion. And what better place? If to travel the world is to encounter the stories that make up the texture of the world, then New York is its library, the place where people come from the world over. I walk the streets of the city, watching football matches in bars with Africans, South Americans, and Europeans; I attend mosques and churches, synagogues and temples; I study Kabbalah with a rabbi, meditation in Chinatown.

We live uptown, in Harlem, in a building that was once the home of Duke Ellington. We can still taste a bit of old New York, before everyone is priced out. This is a Dominican neighborhood, with Latin smells and sounds on every corner. Luis, who now lives in Yonkers, stops by with weed on his way home each night. Sometimes we walk across the bridge to a Yankees game, or down to Rucker Park, where my mother used to watch the Giants play when it was the Polo Grounds. It's Harlem, technically, but its Dominican rhythms were straight Washington Heights. I work on 125th Street, and pass by the African hair braiders each day, the men selling incense and oil; the Garveyites decrying America, Christianity, or anything else; the street preachers summoning the apocalypse, Black Muslims selling *The Final Call*. While I am busy with school, Ari struggles finding purpose; whereas I am inspired by New York's frenetic energy, Ari is stressed.

But we are happy, I think. I am immersed in my studies and my dreams. I never know what demons might have plagued

Ari. But we are so in love. We get a cat and name her Circe, the sorcerer of Greek mythology, laugh as she chases dust and shadows in our little apartment.

After living together for two years in New York, we get married. I will later come to understand that I am not at all ready for it. There is nothing at all in my experiences in life that would have shown me how to be a good husband. We don't know what we're doing; maybe if we had known we wouldn't have done it.

A wedding is at once magical and misleading. It deceives us into thinking that a marriage will be anything like a wedding, when in fact, marriage is defined less by our best days than by our worst. Its magic isn't so much in how beautiful your lover is—that's a bit of a trick. Its magic is in everything else. It is found in the old friends who come, in the families that come together, making new family. But the thing we learn on our wedding night was this: A marriage, a good marriage, is never about just two people. It's about a collision of communities, a commingling of families, an entanglement of friendships and relationships. We came together on a sunny afternoon in June on the side of a mountain in Asheville, North Carolina, to celebrate our love for one another. But what we find is that our love for one another is impossible to separate from any other love we have.

And we need that entanglement.

Home. There are people—I envy them—who have a sense of home in this world, people who know where they belong. I've never belonged anywhere, really. We will move dozens of times, live all over the country, wander all over the world. So what, then, to someone like me, does home even mean? How can one *belong* without a sense of *home*?

But what if home isn't a place? Your ancestors, Ari, were stolen from their home in Africa. Brought to these shores through the quintessential home-eradicating process of the middle passage, then torn from their kin and home again and again through the brutal slave economy, they were tasked with rediscovering home each time. And they did. Acceptance and home-ing—if we can make it into the verb that it truly ought to be—became central to the Black American experience. We all, in these times of collective homelessness, ought to listen to this wisdom.

I may never find a home in the sense that you do on the south side of Chicago, or in the sense that our ancestors, embedded in an autochthonous culture and ecology, did. But perhaps I can find an imperfect sense of belonging in the realization, Ari, that home, for me, is you.

22. CALIFORNIA
2005-2009

Y OU COME AS IF IT WERE A DREAM. *And you are. In you, billions of years of exploding cosmos explode out of womb and into my life. My daughter. Cosima. Cosmos. An entire Universe of wisdom alive in the bloody mess that is my daughter.*

In my memories of these days, I will later reflect, it is always sunny. This is in part, perhaps, the product of the stereotype a northeasterner holds of California. But there are many rainy days, a whole rainy season, in northern California. These memories are more psychological than meteorological. You are the sun, shining in my life.

I never would have imagined how much you would change me. The day you are born I discover both joy and grief I have never really understood before. I know that you are something more beautiful than I have ever known. And even as we'll wander through forests together in later years, even as we'll discuss philosophy and laugh and laugh and laugh, I will always know that this great joy comes with the ultimate sorrow: that there will be a day when you'll go away.

After the wedding and a honeymoon in Europe—a trip that we think will be one of a lifetime of adventure and travel—we move to California, where I continue my studies. It comes to pass that in California I will study other things, too.

First, I come to see that to study "religion" or "philosophy" with any kind of integrity means to study the Universe, the Earth, Nature herself. Words and ideas begin to coalesce around the sense that the world is alive. I fall in love with the great redwoods, the ocean crashing against the rugged Pacific coast. I've returned, finally, to the coast where I camped years before. I fall in love with my daughter. And like all love stories, it radicalizes me. I see that we are killing her world.

And I also come to study *studying*. That is, I begin to see that this great killing is rooted in a story of *loneliness*. A lie. And the only way past the lie is to re-learn how to be human. To re-learn how to learn. You see, everything is education, everywhere a school. When we choose to build a prison or raise an army, we haven't taken money away from education—we've chosen to educate in a different way, through a different lens—*tell a different story*. For the most important thing the educator does isn't the skills or knowledge passed on; it's the metaphor for the world that's created.

I have several great teachers—in addition to the Redwoods—during my time in California. Matthew Fox is a former priest, kicked out by the Vatican partly for believing in the rights of women and gays, but mostly for believing in the sacredness of creation.

I study with Matt and we begin to discuss the possibility of teaching young people in the same way that he has been teaching his graduate students. Matt has developed a unique pedagogical approach, one that involves not merely the intellect, but the integration of intellect, body, and soul—and, perhaps most significantly, creativity. He has partnered with a local rapper and harpist, "Professor Pitt", who plans to make music videos with the kids. But when Matt and Pitt fall out, I take over. I turn Matt's ideas into something the kids can relate to.

I ask them to tell their stories.

I watch the news every night as Katrina ravages New Orleans. Our resources depleted with a series of foreign wars, we learn what we already knew: that Black lives do not matter in America. We learn that, while we fight over oil and religion, the seas are rising up to meet us, and we had better learn to swim. I cannot sleep at night as the images of people lined up outside the Superdome, crying out from their rooftops for help, plays out in my mind. They will drown, some of them, like the ancestors who leapt from slave ships, or those who tried to cross rivers, looking for freedom.

America is something like a great Noah's Ark for white people. But, perhaps, there is more to the story. Perhaps, like the Icarus of my imagination, like Dante as he descends into the inferno, the real story only happens after they fall into the depths. Perhaps it is not Noah and his parade of nuclear families, but they extended families that were left behind in the rising waters.

News comes more quickly now than when I lived in Africa. But some news still travels slowly. Denise's story comes as a whisper. To cope with unimaginable trauma, she is now on medication that swells her little body up to enormous proportions. It is hard to recognize the little girl I once tossed in the air. She, like the world itself, has become so heavy.

Other news comes even slower. I discover that Mattie has died, unexpectedly, still young but exhausted. The four she's taken in are orphans again. But not really. Ottie, of course, takes them in.

I still speak to Antonio regularly, although we rarely see one another. An argument that had started twenty years before continues. Class and race and the possibilities for American reconciliation. He loves and hates America with equal fury, just as he loves and hates his own people. He is looking, always: both for answers and for his own voice. He sees, all around him, every day, things that white people—and the Black bourgeoisie—can have that he cannot. But over the course of twenty years I begin to see that he has a unique and creative capability to deal with this injustice without succumbing to insanity—he, like all of us, is only partly there—or, worse, becoming boring.

He converts to Judaism. This is part protest, part reclamation project, part spiritual search. If white people can be Jews, why can't he? His theory on this is not far from that of groups like the Black Hebrew Israelites, who claim that Black people are the real Jews of the Bible. But he wants to be part of a white synagogue—all the while clinging to his unique identity as the Black Jew. He tortures the liberal, suburban Synagogue with his presence. They don't consider him a Jew, of course, but they are too liberal to actually kick him out.

After numerous discussions on the subject, he finally confesses to me that he's in love with his rabbi. "There is always some kind of romance with you, man," I tell him. "Complex historical and philosophical and political arguments and then it just turns out you want to bang the rabbi."

"Well," he says. "I do like Jewish chicks."

He insists that this is more. True love. But things, unsurprisingly, go sour.

He then takes a trip to Tunisia to recover his Moorish roots. He gets in way over his head, winds up sharing a flat with some migrants from Sub-Saharan Africa and, finally, running out of money and fleeing to Provence. He calls me to get some money wired to get home, complaining of how racist those damn Arabs are.

It is in an early morning phone call—before texts and Facebook—that I learn of my brother's cancer. He's worked so hard to find his way in life. He is back in Rochester now, with a wife and a son and another on the way. He's gotten in shape and developed a hernia while lifting weights. When they open him up, they find the cancer.

It's hopeless, really. There is never any chance. They tear his body apart over and over again. There is only one unspoken purpose: to allow him to live long enough for his sons to remember him.

Strangely, this event—cancer—that surely is the worst thing that has ever happened to him, gives him a purpose he's always lacked. My brother, timid in many ways, faces it with a fierce and stoic courage. This is the thing he teaches me: There is integrity in fighting a lost cause. He, like our world, seems to have little hope. But he endures the eviscerating surgeries, the toxic medications, in order to do one thing: to live a little longer in order to have his sons remember him, and to show them how to die. This is the lesson we all need to learn on a dying planet. It's the only way our children can save us.

But the most significant event for me in California is that I become a father. Fatherhood in this world is difficult, for the world conspires against the one thing our children need more than anything: being fully human. Everything is sterile, two-dimensional. She has inherited from us a world without texture, a world lived on screens, without depth. *How, I wonder, can I teach her to fall in love?*

But at the same time, children offer something we cannot access without them. *They play.* They make worlds every day, then take them apart, reimagine them, and begin again.

Seeing the world through my daughter's eyes is to recognize that play is the source of all worldmaking. Childhood is the original adventure.

And perhaps this is what I was always looking for in my travels—the adventure of childhood.

And so, there, in California, I find it. That thing that I have been searching for, that question that I've been unable to ask. Family. Home. Intimacy. It turns out that it was not to be found in the freedom of the road or in the stars, but in days passing by, slowly in the California sun, cooking and sharing food, changing a diaper, camping in the Redwoods. A first word or step, the bed in the morning, each morning, Ari, Cosima, and me. And it is the thing that I always feared finding; for, once found, it can be lost.

Ari has been away from Chicago for nearly a decade. We are happy, but something is missing for her, something I cannot really understand. She wants to be closer to her people, feels some connection to a specific place that I never will. So we leave the California sun, the Redwoods, the sea, and return to the middle of the continent, to where we started, only blocks from the porch where I met her, so many years before, shining in the late afternoon sun.

23. CHICAGO

2009-2019

I RETURN TO CHICAGO, FINALLY, IN 2009, AS A FATHER. I have degrees and have published a small volume of poetry. I have ideas, too. The job market, however, for "philosopher-poet" is not so good. So I create a non-profit, a vehicle to teach and to re-imagine education. It grows beyond what I've imagined possible, beyond what I even want. We buy land and take groups of young people into the woods to camp, to look at the stars. They are amazed at the nighttime sky, like I was in Africa or in the Middle Eastern desert. We are looking for spaces where they can feel the texture of the world again, re-imagining themselves and re-telling their stories.

Dee's story has continued without me, of course. He has been released from jail. While I was away, Winston worked for him, finding him a lawyer, bringing attention to his case, until they finally let him out after nearly a year behind bars. I see him every now and then on the streets. He tells me how they drugged him, saying he was mentally ill, and how that was why they said he killed his mother. We'll talk for a bit, remembering the old days, before everything, then move on.

I visit the Children's Center from time to time, too. Sue is on her way out the door. The dementia has increased to the point that she can no longer really be in charge of the Center—or even herself. She's stopped driving, and now, when she no longer comes to Sue—to the place that in more than name was her *self*—she will sit by the door each day, awaiting a ride that she can't remember no longer comes. A board is formed—bankers and business-people—to take over the center, to *professionalize* it.

Still, some Sue kids join my new program. Serenity is among them. The little girl who once ate apples from my hand is growing into adolescence and developing a mind and a spirit to question everything.

I write books about how we might find intimacy in the vast and lonely cosmos, about lonely men—like me—wandering in the world. My organization grows. I am loved, and there is much to tell about all this work. But slowly it becomes apparent that this is not the real story. This isn't my real work. The real work was the thing I ran from all those years: family.

The mere fact of the existence of my children is a lesson in the miraculous. Out of nothing—out of us—they are here. One moment quivering and gasping for breath, the next reading novels and building forts, the next writing novels and building bridges. They can see, in their own newness, the freshness and newness of the world. We think, sometimes, that we've seen it all. But the world is born new and fresh every day—and this is a bloody and messy process. Through the eyes of a child, we can see this.

This is their gift to me. I can never repay it.

The world conspires against listening, and listening is the one thing each parent must do. So parenting is a practice, primarily, of mindfulness. It asks me, each day, to pay attention. A child—even a single child—demands this of the world: *pay attention*. This is the thing we seem least able to do in the modern world.

If we can be mindful, we not only give our child the one gift they really crave, we also can become aware of the miraculousness of existence. We become aware of the worlds they create each day. We become aware of the novelty of every moment, perceiving the gift that they bring us: the capacity to find joy and beauty in our world.

Finally, we become aware of the closest thing that I have experienced to what Christians call "grace": I can make a thousand mistakes—I *do* make a thousand mistakes, sometimes before breakfast—and still I receive immeasurable, unconstrained love. We are all given a family. A thing, static. A noun. But this is perhaps a more Western conception of family, rooted in the rigid absolutes of genetics and the modern nuclear family. But other people have long known that a family is something made in relationship.

Ari and I share something in our marriage: Loneliness in childhood. Whom do I trust to care for me, to know me? The answer to this is in the experiences we made, together—family. Heaven, for me, is a morning in the bed. The children come in, first the little ones, then Cosima, to cuddle. All five of us, together, a single body. *Love.*

I am willing to do anything for Ari. And I do. That is, anything except ask her what she wants.

Ari and I work together with teens for years. We bring them into our home, take them on retreats. Make family with them. She is the only one who believes in me in the beginning, and I will never forget it. She knows my books will be genius, knows I'll take this thing—my "wisdom project"—and change the world with it. She comes to all the book events when they are sparsely attended, girls in tow. She stays at home while I sit writing in some café, day after day.

We teach together, run retreats and camps together. It is the great joy of my life: my little children and wife by my side as this thing I birthed, dreamed up, grows. Together, we teach and mentor dozens of teens.

I am good at big ideas and teaching, bad at everything else: raising money, hiring and firing, keeping the books. But somehow it works. People give me money, believe in me. When they praise me, when I win an award or two, I believe it all and want more. Ari is still there, still working alongside me. But when everyone else praises me, and not her, her praise for me becomes less frequent. And then our funding temporarily dries up. I focus on writing and teaching. Even when we regain funding, the youth programming shifts to Baltimore. There is no longer a place for her.

Ari has shrunk herself for me from the beginning. She loved me so much, you see, that she tried to make herself into what she thought I wanted. And she has lost herself in me. I was oblivious to this, couldn't comprehend her despair, so captivated was I with my mission, my work, my ambition—my belief in my own goodness.

I visit Sue at her daughter's house. They've brought her here to die, but of course she won't. Stubborn even in death. She can barely speak, but there seems to be some glimmer of recognition in her. I bring her children, "Sue kids" who are now grown, some with children of their own. We watch her, talk to her, as she struggles to eat, as she shits on herself. She's always favored the Romantics, and used to write out poems she particularly loved. Two poems still sit on my desk, after all these years. The first is Dylan Thomas:

> Do not go gentle into that good night,
> Old age should burn and rave at close of day;
> Rage, rage against the dying of the light.

Her youngest son has been running the center, but he steps down from the position just as I lose my biggest funder and we are struggling with money. There are some who think I should apply. *Why not me?*

When Sue is told that I may take over, she claps her hands. *She remembers.*

But The Sue Duncan Children's Center is now controlled by a board of directors made up of bankers and financiers. In her incapacity, they will professionalize the center, make it flat and replicable and quantifiable. *Remove its texture.* They'll get those kids to know what time it is in the global economy, just like the Danish NGO, turn them into bankers—if not, there is the military or prison. I interview with them, this committee of bankers. They've established a rubric to determine the successor. They are seeking metrics, not memories. I have no chance. They reject me.

The other poem on my desk, in Sue's hand, is Yeats:

Things fall apart; the centre cannot hold;
Mere anarchy is loosed upon the world,
The blood-dimmed tide is loosed, and everywhere
The ceremony of innocence is drowned;
The best lack all conviction, while the worst
Are full of passionate intensity.

The end times are all around us—in our politics, our literature, our arts. We watch the apocalypse unfold on the news each night. I can see it because I've walked around the planet, because I've felt the texture of this world. Because I haven't looked away. Like my brother, I have to teach this to my children.

As the earth warms, the seas rise, and the forests burn, there is a deeper apocalypse at hand: The flattening of the world, its becoming two dimensions, without depth. The work that my ATM-installer friend started is nearly complete. But my wandering is part of the cure. I have learned to be comfortable with the absurdity of this new story, with multiple, contradictory stories. I have learned, from all those I've encountered, that all those stories have to be heard. The suppression of those alternative stories, the genocide not merely of peoples but of worldviews, like the suppression of the world's biodiversity, is killing us.

I can see, though, that I have to love the world, flawed and sorrowful as it is, in order to uncover those stories.

The banker and the engineer—the high priests of capitalism—have conspired to rob us of our depth, our soul, of the texture of our world. I have to teach my girls to fight the tyranny of the screen.

One night, Vismaya comes downstairs after being awakened by gunshots—a not-altogether-uncommon experience where we live. Are we safe? she asks. *Yes, baby,* I say. *I will keep you safe.*

I realize now that good parenting requires us to be liars:

We tell our children that the world is essentially good, that hard work and decency are rewarded, tell them that we are strong enough to keep them safe, that things will get better, that the joy will outweigh the pain, good will overcome evil. We tell them that those gunshots they heard won't touch them, that those racists will die off and their hate will evaporate, that our ingenuity will clean our air and water.

We teach them that if they love enough, that if they fight for what is right and good, their world will be better than ours, better than the world they were given.

We tell them that if they love hard enough, they will be loved back.

The lie comes in many forms: We call it heaven, or justice, or progress. We call it love, too. But whatever we call it, being a good parent requires that we love our children more than we trust all the evidence before us. Because we could never forgive ourselves for bringing them into this world as we know it. So we invent a world, a lie, a fantasy that protects them, in part, but mostly it protects us.

All our lullabies allow us to sleep at night, not them.

We lie to them because we believe, somehow, in spite of all the evidence handed down to us by our ancestors, that our love is strong enough for them to make it become the truth.

Our children—especially Cosima—see us at our best and at our worst. Through drunkenness and fighting and absolute despair. They witness us failing each other and them.

Cosima, because she is the oldest, sometimes will ask me—with only a look—if everything is okay.

Yes, baby, I will take care.

And I flounder with this. Playing the hero but enabling. Pretending that *I* am okay when I'm not.

Vismaya brings us a picture one night after a fight. Ari and me and her, smiling in front of a happy home. These are the things that break your heart, make you feel utterly unworthy.

And they also give you the courage to confront your demons.

At some point, most parents have to decide whether to shield their children from the harsh realities of our world or to allow them to retain some innocence of childhood. In the film La Bella Vita, *this question is taken to the absurd: a father, Guido, and his son are taken to a concentration camp and Guido convinces his son that it's all a game. In the age of polycrisis, we are all Guido at some point.*

Cosima often will complain about how overprotective the Black parents are on the south side where we live. For generations, we explain, Black people in America had to discipline and protect their children with an understanding that America was a place in which they were never safe beyond Black family and community.

And now, as parents, we have brought children, perhaps, into a dying world, or at least a collapsing civilization. What are the skills they require? Certainly, a mistake we might make would be to assume that the credentials of a collapsing system would be of value. Perhaps they need survival skills, like growing food or shooting a gun (or bow and arrow). But maybe the best thing to do to confront the apocalypse as parents is to acknowledge the most obvious aspect of the transition: We do not know.

My intuition is that our children need to know how to love, how to be in community, how to look within and cry together. This is as important as growing food. It is food.

At times, I mourn the world into which I have brought them. And it's not even really the destruction of it. It's the sterility. I wish they could get lost. I wish they could travel the world without being tethered to a smartphone, without a map.

24. SUE: "A PRISON"

I HAVE ONLY EVER VISITED SUE AT HER HOUSE. And really, I've rarely ever seen her anywhere other than her house or the Children's Center. Only in worlds of her making. Messy places.

Now, I am standing in the lobby of the assisted care facility that is her new home. Cosima is there with me. She knows Sue, has seen her many times. But I have to explain and re-explain the idea of Alzheimer's.

The building is fine, I guess. It's sterile. There is security. The guard is polite and business-like. He is the opposite of Marsha.

When we reach the room, Sue is lying down, semi-conscious, on the sofa in her room. Ottie sits in a chair next to her. Ottie comes every day, Ottie who is a great grandmother and who still cares for her adopted children, and for their children, comes every day to care for Sue, to see if she can get her to eat something. Sue's breakfast is getting cold.

Ottie greets me warmly. She says hi to Cosima, who waves shyly. Cosima is a shy child, at times, and she senses the absurdity of this place, of Sue's presence there.

Sue's daughter has tried to bring her into her home, but Sue escaped. She's become impossible to care for. She's fallen and injured herself. She won't take medication. No one wanted her to be sent here. There are, in many cases, no good choices to be made, only bad ones. Sue understands this much, at least.

Ottie tells Sue I am there, in her room. She awakes from her reverie and looks around the room. She seems to recognize me. She will recognize me long after she's forgotten many others. I was central to her work, there every day. There is nothing that defines her more. I explain that Cosima is my daughter. Her eyes go wide. I pull out a photo from my pocket. My family. I point to the people in the photo, explaining who they are. She asks what I am doing with my life. I say that I am writing, that I work with teens to give them the chance to tell their story. She nods—in approval, I think.

"This place," she says, "They've got me in a prison here."

I can only nod sadly as Cosima squirms uncomfortably. Sue smiles at her, the instinct to tune into the little ones still there. Cosima softens. Sue looks around for a toy or pinecone, something to give her. But there is nothing. This place is too clean. Sue stares off for a moment, as if she's lost to us again.

"Are you coming to the center today?" she asks.

25. DEATH BED
2013

We are talking about sports when the doorbell rings. My brother's wife gets it. She always gets it.

"We've got a bed here," says the man at the door.

"Oh," she says, "we thought you were coming at six. They told us six."

"Six? Wonder why they said that?" The man pauses, kindly, to allow for the woman in front of him to recognize that he understands the significance of the bed. He's done this before. "Sorry about the mix up, but, well, we've got the bed. Can we come in?"

"Yes, yes. Of course."

We have to stop talking about sports. The bed and all it represents has insinuated itself.

The two men carry parts and explain things about the bed, its assembly and operation, to anyone who will listen. They make an uncomfortable amount of eye contact with me while my brother, dying and emaciated, waits. They put it together in front of us, as my brother seems to be falling apart, held together with blankets, tubes and drugs.

"Can we put it right here?" they ask, still looking at me. It will be in front of the TV, in front of the football game we'd been discussing. I—the only one in the room who does not live there, who is not clearly dying or married to a dying man—say nothing. "That's fine," says my brother's wife.

Bed between TV and us, there is now only the subject of death. Its various humiliations become the topic of discussion. The only topic possible. They begin to explain the bed's attributes to my brother and me. I try not to look rudely indifferent while conveying that my brother should be the one to whom they are speaking. *He's not gone yet*, I want to say. *He still exists and still can control a fucking bed*. But they continue to explain it all to me. Finally, they come to the rails on the side. I remember the bed my brother had as a child, after he'd outgrown his crib but there was still concern he'd fall out in his sleep. These railings can be adjusted, the man explains, through some process I don't follow.

"Can we just take them off?" says my brother. He wants to say, but cannot, that he is not going to roll out of his bed. He is a dying man, not a child.

"Yeah, sure," says the man. He is not unkind. *He must hate coming into this kind of home*, I think, *the kind where the dying man is young and the pitter-patter of his children's feet rather than the dull drone of the home shopping network provide the background for his work*. I feel a moment of compassion and admiration for his job: *The Deliverer of Deathbeds*.

Mercifully, he leaves. My brother's youngest son comes in and looks uncomprehendingly at the bed. "What's this?" he asks.

"It's a new bed for daddy," says my brother with a smile. "It will help me sleep better. So my back won't hurt." The euphemisms, so long practiced, slide off his tongue so easily that they—unburdened with the agony of the truth—have become themselves something like truth, true in the strange bubble that has become their home, the home of a dying man.

"Why is it here?" he asks. Four-year-olds are more honest. More direct.

"We should move it," says my brother. "It's really in the way."

And the little boy nods, walking thoughtfully away.

26. IN MY FORTIETH YEAR
2013

In my fortieth year, something remarkable happens. A girl, my second daughter, Calliope, is born. She is a big girl, with big, bright, thoughtful eyes that will only grow brighter as she grows. Five days later, my brother dies. I leave the little girl, along with her mother and her big sister, behind in Chicago as I travel back to Rochester to bury my brother. All forty years are woven into this journey. It is the time when memories begin slowly to overtake my dreams, that moment that Dante called, in those famous first lines of the *Commedia*, "*il mezzo del cammin di nostra vita*"—the middle of the journey of our life. I am indeed entering, as Dante did, the "*selva oscura*"—the dark wood. The question is now, for me as it was for him, *would the straight way be lost?*

A week before, I came to Rochester to see him on his deathbed, having gotten word that he had little time left. I flew on a Saturday afternoon and arrived on a dreary, autumnal day, long shadows barely visible through the misty rain. He said nothing as I arrived, but seemed to slowly take me into focus as I entered his room. He spoke in a near-whisper, but I was relieved that something of him was still there, even as his body had deteriorated beyond recognition. This once-giant of a man weighed a mere 130 pounds, all skin and bones. But he still could talk, still had the same wit, the same sharp sense of humor. We talked about bullshit for a while. He came in and out of consciousness, his wife filling in the gaps.

"This is all I got, Teddy," he told me. I said nothing, then he added, "This is hard. So hard." I didn't ask, and continued to wonder long after, whether he meant the mere dying—the pain, the sickness, the suffering—or the life he was leaving behind.

He felt nauseous; I was asked to leave so he could vomit. In time, I came back into the room. He pulled me close to him and told me what a good brother I'd been, what a good role-model. I felt none of this to be true. I wept and told him how proud I was of *him*. It had indeed been hard, but he'd been so brave. Timid in all other things, my brother was courageous in death.

I return for the funeral alone. My little girl is too small for the journey, and Ari's mother comes to help out with the girls. Somehow, this seems like a trip I can only make alone anyway.

It is decided that there will be a public visitation, followed, the next day, by a burial at which I will speak. My father can do little in the way of speaking about this, at least speaking deeply, nor can he comfort my mother. Afraid, perhaps, of the depth of his own emotion, he remains silent. My brother's death is an even clearer boundary crossing for him than for me. It marks the end of his professional life. He will be defined, it seems to me, as an old man who's buried his son, rather than by the work he did. This is a strange development for a man who's always defined himself through his work, who has always felt truly only comfortable at the office.

They come by the hundreds. Many of my brother's buddies from high school, and still more of my friends; parents of friends; people from the neighborhood; my fifth grade teacher; my junior high basketball coach; my pediatrician. Strange apparitions, all of them, old and wrinkled versions of themselves. "Hi, Ted," they say. I stare until they explain: "I'm Mr so-and-so." They never say, "an older-wrinkled-version of Mr So-and-so," but it is clear they are. "Yes," I respond cheerfully—and I am genuinely happy to see them all—"Of course you are." I don't say, "I didn't recognize you because I could have sworn that Mr So-and-so was younger, larger, more substantial." In a blink-of-an-eye, they have all shrunk and grown old. And my brother is dead, just as Calliope is born.

They buzz around and shake my hand tearfully, telling me how sorry they are. And they mean it. But all I can think of is this: What will I tell Calliope, who will never know her uncle, about him? What kind of person, what kind of man, was he? What did he do with this blink-of-an-eye, this little bit of time—even the luckiest among us only get that—that he got?

I go out later with old East High friends, have drinks and listen to Antonio and Fatima debate the Black middle class.

The next day is the burial, the saddest day of my life. I walk out onto the driveway with my father. "Where's your mother?" he says. "What's she doing?" He makes no effort to go find her, perhaps fearing that, in finding her, she will need comfort he cannot give. I go inside to find her with a book, *Sylvester and the Magic Pebble*. It was Matthew's favorite when he was little. It is the story of a donkey named Sylvester who accidentally turns himself into a stone. I remember my mother crying each time she read it to us at the part where Sylvester's parents cannot find him after he is turned to stone by the magic pebble. My brother, I am told, had been able to repeat the entire story to our pediatrician on his fourth birthday.

My mother is sitting silently with the book in hand, unable to move.

"Are you having a hard time, mom?" I ask softly.

She nods and bursts into tears. I hold her and we weep together. There is something ineffable that we share together, the knowing of mothers and sons, held only between the two of us now.

No one else speaks at the burial but me. I say some words, words that somehow feel like they only serve the purpose of filling the sad and empty air. It is a beautiful day. Strange. I expected rain. I speak of the hardness and shortness of life, of this little blink-of-an-eye we all get, of the pursuit of a good life, of my brother's life being good, and joyful, in spite of all his suffering. The words fill the heavy silence as we place flowers on his ashes. "He can see the library," my mother tells Matt's wife. My brother always liked books. I hold her and we cry together, standing over *Sylvester and the Magic Pebble*. In that book, the stone turns back into a donkey. There will be no such miracle for my brother. The miracle is that, after this little, unlikely flash of life, he could come to cherish and love life, that after so much suffering, something of him endures, not in stone, but in all those who have come to remember.

It was a good life.

In my fortieth year, everything changes. I was born in 1973, in this city, this city that would die a slow death over the course of my lifetime, like other post-industrial towns. I've left, gone as far away as I could possibly go—so far, in fact, that I somehow discovered my own aliveness, in my twenty-fifth year, in a bathroom at the edge of the world, in Mozambique; so far that I learned that the end of the journey took back to the beginning, that what I've always really wanted was the thing that I'd run from. And now, I've returned. The parents of the children I grew up with are here, stooped and gray and barely recognizable. Old friends, too, some who'd gone off like me, others who'd stayed. I speak of my brother and I comfort others, even as I can barely hold it together myself. I become the comforter and the ritualist, not yet an elder, but no longer the young man who wandered the world: I am a father with a growing family; my days of wandering have ended. I return not just to Rochester, but also to the world, to share what I've learned from beyond.

I can see, all around me, ghosts of my past, feel, with my brother's death, a world that is dying. How can I keep my brother alive, the world alive, so they can endure, somehow, in the memories of my children? *I have to remember*; I have to tell my stories, stories of my days of wandering, before the world had lost its texture.

I remember leaving my own lonely bed, when I was little, and sleeping on the floor next to my brother. What was I looking for? Perhaps it was some relief from the terror of the vast and lonely cosmos—a thing called family. It's funny how people are: sometimes the thing that they want most is the thing that they run from the fastest. And when I finally decide that this is what I always wanted, I really don't know how to do it.

After my brother dies, things unravel. A baby is born in our bathroom, unexpected and beautiful; the country descends into chaos; funding sources for my work dry up. Ari and I are entangled, beautifully and impossibly, and cannot find ourselves. I have spent a lifetime flying to the sun: first in seeking adventure, then seeking success. But now I find myself falling, like Icarus, like Vismaya as she left Ari's womb and plunged toward that toilet. I caught her. But the question still remains: who will catch me?

27. OUR WINTER IN MIAMI

2021

> *"Requited or unrequited, to love is to move between homecoming and exile."*
> —DAVID WHYTE

It's the middle of the night, and I am on the highway, heading toward the coast, toward Boca Raton. I've left my daughters and Mariposa's daughter alone at the house, my twelve-year-old in charge.

These are the thoughts I have as I careen down the empty highway: I remember past lives, when I was alone, really alone, and how I always sought starry nights and empty beaches, and here I am, so many years later, heading toward ocean and nighttime sky. *I had always thought I was heading toward the stars, but now I know that I am falling into the sea.* I remember thousands of kindnesses and failures in a marriage that has lasted for fifteen years and produced three children. I remember everything, and nothing, as I drive. I have an address in my GPS, but I have no idea where I am going.

I pass through the town of Parkland. Stoneman Douglass High School, a great white box against the dark sky, shines bright in the moonlight, contrasted like death and sorrow against suburban numbness, like the coldness of it all in the warm, subtropical night.

I call my wife on the highway. It makes no sense. I am coming to get her, coming to argue with her, anyway. But I feel like I need to hear her voice, like somehow it will reassure me, like somehow I won't make it if she isn't talking to me. After all of it, her voice is the sound of *home*. Her drunken words slur and she hangs up.

I get confused in Boca Raton, can't find the place. My thoughts are muddled and unfocused. I call again. Her friend, Mariposa, who's home she's at, guides me to her apartment.

There are three of them in front of the complex and I pull up, prepared to take my wife home. Prepared also to be chastised for leaving a child, for showing up in the middle of the night like this.

But instead, Mariposa asks if I'm OK.

No, I answer, disoriented by the contrast of her kindness and my own despair. *I love my family*.

Maybe you shouldn't drive. She says. Why don't you come inside?

I don't know what to say. I can't think. I sit on a curb and begin to cry. Keeda, who's been friends with my wife for decades, who surely, I think, will be annoyed or angry at me for showing up like this, puts her hand gently on my shoulder. I realize, at that moment, that I haven't been taken care of by anyone in years, maybe decades. That I was always taking care of everyone else around me. Or so I thought. I think of my mother. I want my mother. I want to go home, but no longer know what that means.

Mariposa walks me upstairs and sits me down. She begins to tell me about her family, her struggles, stories that I barely can comprehend but serve to let me know: *I'm not alone*. She pauses meaningfully. Can I speak plainly? she asks.

It's the only kind of talking I can understand, I say.

You know she's depressed, right? she says.

As recently as one hundred and fifty years ago, south Florida would be hardly recognizable. Citrus plantations and alligators, sabal palm and southern oak, but little that resembled the modern multicultural metropolis of Miami or the splendor of South Beach. South Florida was a backwater then, a place that one might escape to, as many enslaved African people did in their sporadic alliance with the Seminole. Eventually, both these groups were pushed out as white people established and developed Miami. Native plants were replaced along with native people, brackish water invading the water supply with each string of summer storms. But still, people came. Even the white southerner would be replaced by retirees and sun chasers from the northeast. We are a stubborn species: we'll keep loving or hating despite what the world shows us.

Miami is a place of contradictions. It's in the south, but not really Southern. It is a diverse cosmopolis that votes Republican. There is something fake about it, its delusional denial of the encroaching sea, the plastic surgery. And still, it was here that we came to find something as real as long days playing in the sunshine, of beaches. We came to Miami in our own web of contradictions, too. It was winter, and yet it was hot and sunny. But something about it was as wintry, cold and dark as the Chicago we'd left.

We came to Miami to find some sunshine in the winter, and more winters than one, not just the brutal cold of Chicago, but the dark winter of the second year of the pandemic. We came to Miami to grow our bubble—our children could play with Mariposa's children, and we could be around other adults, too. What we hadn't realized was that this was the winter of our lives, that we brought not only the desire to find some sunshine for a few months, but that we needed to find someone to share our scars with.

My marriage, and my life, are falling apart.

The narrative that the pandemic is causing our problems is easy, but false. The pandemic is a light turning on. It had been easy to move through life in denial. But here it is. There's nowhere to go; it's impossible to hide from myself.

We decide that what's in order is some sunshine. So, as the second winter of the pandemic lockdown approaches, we pack up and go to Miami. We leave the cold, the snow, and the darkness behind. We think we'll leave our troubles, too, but that isn't how it works. Stowaways in our souls since childhood, they had little trouble finding their way into our packed car.

But we are at least starting to follow a dream, a dream we've always held, then lost, like so many other dreams—life had come along and snatched us up. It had seemed, in the early days, like we'd always be able to travel—Ari believed I'd show her the world, and I believed it, too.

But shit gets complicated. We move and I go back to school. I have ambitions and little money. I am a struggling writer, a social entrepreneur starting a nonprofit from scratch, an adjunct professor. We have children. At first, just one, then another, followed quickly by a third surprise baby. There is always my work, a lack of money, a little baby or toddler at home. I wake up every day wondering when there would be more, wondering how life became such drudgery.

I pick up my *New York Times* every Sunday morning from my stoop and think of Henry Hill, in witness protection yearning for the adventure of his youth.

Ari goes inside, to a deep and dark place that I couldn't reach. She blames me. And I blame myself.

I bring Ari home that night, in spite of it all. For a moment, a brief moment, it seems like perhaps we won't go home together, that we would, at least for a night and maybe longer, part ways. But somehow, we can't.

I can't sleep for the first few nights; and when I can, I have nightmares, visions of loss, the thing that had scared me the whole time, my greatest fear, emerging in the night: The fear that my family was coming apart, the fear of loneliness, the thing that had always been my worst nightmare.

Words come forth after that, first angry words, then, for the first time ever, real and honest ones. We tell each other about our fears, our sorrow. Thoughts pour out that were so terrifying that we never could have admitted them, even to ourselves.

The sun shines so brightly each day. Our children play all day, learn to swim, climb trees. We read books and tell stories. Some days, we awake early and go to the ocean, swimming with the rising sun.

We start to learn this, slowly at first, then with a deluge as the words pour forth: A marriage is a thing we made together, her story and my story commingling, co-creating a family, a home, together.

Mariposa and her daughter come several times a week.

I think it was meant to be, she says, smiling. Mariposa has a way of saying things that are sad and profound, but, coming from her, sound funny. We are all struggling, she goes on, with some of the same shit. And now, here we are, together.

You should write a book about it, she continues.

Ari laughs and cringes.

I laugh and say, *I think I will.* They look at me, wondering if I'm serious.

There are many things to learn from the place at which I have arrived. But the first lesson is that there is no greater gift than family, and that no grievance is worth losing it. So, I have work to do. I have to learn to forgive myself. But to do so I have to figure out how I got here, and why. And to do that, I have to go back and tell my story, a process not merely of creation, but of *excavation*.

28. ON LONGING & BELONGING

2021

Nel mezzo del cammin di nostra vita mi ritrovai
per una selva oscura, ché la diritta via era smarrita.

In the middle of the journey of our life
I found myself within a dark forest,
For the straightforward pathway had been lost.

—DANTE'S *COMMEDIA*, CANTO I, LINES 1-3

THIS LONELY APOCALYPSE ISN'T JUST ABOUT BURNING FORESTS AND RISING SEAS. It's a story of disembodiment and disconnection. It started long before it all began to fall apart. The Israelites knew it when they told their stories of collective liberation; the Buddhists knew it when they told stories of interconnection. Quantum physicists know it today, even if they don't fully grasp the consequences. My daughters know it.

What we are all after isn't some disembodied and sterile eternity, the kind promised by fundamentalist preachers and tech-bros. What we are looking for is community. *Our world isn't a collection of things, or even of people. It's* story. *It's* relationship. *When we see that, we can fall in love with the world.*

This beautiful entanglement is the thing I'd been looking for since I was a little boy, contemplating the vast and empty cosmos. If only I'd know that it wasn't the edge of the universe I'd been peering into, but the edge of my own soul.

Dante excluded, no one tells you about the dark forest, the struggle of middle age. Sure, there are the clichés about leaving your wife for the secretary, your husband for the gardener. But none of this really gets to the heart of the matter—*the dark forest*. For me, it begins right after I turn forty, with the death of my brother and the birth of my second child.

Our lives only get harder from there. There is another child, that cosmic surprise born in our bathroom. Now there are three children, not to mention a nineteen-year-old niece, neither in school nor working, living in our basement. The funding for my nonprofit dries up; teaching and writing opportunities dissipate. I pour my energy into my children. Feeling forgotten and aimless, Ari goes into a dark place. She plays things over and over in her head: A childhood in which she was sometimes harmed and seldom heard. She begins to see these things all around her.

As her forty-third birthday approaches, Ari is playing something else over and over in her head: She is only eighteen years old; her father is forty-three, living in Las Vegas. It is late and night and he is driving down a long and empty road. He is drunk, tired. He nods. His car swerves into an oncoming car, killing him. Like her father, she has feelings she doesn't want to feel, and focuses her energies on keeping them at bay.

When I was a child, I was always the independent son, the one who didn't need extra help. The one who was okay, while my brother wasn't. And I could protect and save those who needed it. I was a hero in all my own stories even before I became a writer. I worked with marginalized youth for years, a hero in the community who could cross you over in our open gyms, who could go up the school and meet with your teachers, who'd pick you up from jail or the hospital, or who'd help you move when you got evicted.

And now, with my wife at home depressed, I could be the hero in my family, too. It would have been easy to blame her for being too tired to deal with the kids in the morning. But who, you might ask, made the drinks last night? Was it the same guy making breakfast now?

The pandemic is the first light. It becomes impossible not to see that our marriage is in trouble, to realize that Ari is depressed. We fight, and drink, and make love. We relearn how to love each other every night, then forget, then remember again. We drink away the spring and summer on our front porch, laughing and crying, deluding ourselves in isolation.

As spring rolls on, it becomes clear that the pandemic is only getting worse. Ari feels like a prisoner. Then George Floyd is murdered and city and after city burns. Smoke fills our porch at night, sirens blaring and helicopters circling, protestors and looters commingling, men and women running past our house each night, trash bags filled with loot. We go to protests, but mostly watch the uprising on the internet and through the screened-in porch. One night someone breaks through our screen, another there's a firebombing at the end of the block, still another a stolen car crash. Gunshots, unencumbered by six-foot-social-distancing, pierce the summer night as unemployment soars.

I always wake up first, Ari hungover in the bed, and cook breakfast. Then I sit on the porch, listening to love songs, thinking about George Floyd and my wife, my children. *He called for his dead mother.* I cannot shake this. He cried out for her, as he was murdered in front of the whole world, a world that now burns in rage and sorrow. This shatters me. And I, too, burn in rage and sorrow. I cry every morning—for a world on fire, for my wife and children. For George Floyd, the man who, with his last, dying breath, called out for his dead mother.

We are sitting by the pool now. The cool nights of January and February—yes, even in Miami a winter night can be cool—have faded into warmth. The younger children are in bed; the oldest is talking to her friends on the phone. There are stars here, on the edge of the Everglades.

I am thinking about the loneliness of childhood. It is a thing we share, Ari and me—the loneliness of our past. Whereas Ari can point to certain traumatic events and circumstances, there was nothing terribly traumatic for me that I can point to. I was just lonely; I just didn't quite fit. But I learned, quickly and with some skill, that I could find my place when I could take care of someone else. I learned that if I could fly, if I could touch the stars, I'd be loved—or at least admired enough to pretend I was loved—enough to stave off the loneliness. I was like Gilgamesh, building walls because they'd keep me safe; like Gilgamesh, I thought I could be a god. But also like Gilgamesh, I needed to learn to be human, to fall, to die, to be more like his friend Enkidu, the wild man. I needed the depths, not the stars.

The clearest lessons in life are never explicit; any decent educator will tell you that. There was much I learned in my childhood, good as well as bad. But I would not realize until

I got to Miami that I had been taught that my role in this world was to be needed rather than to have needs. These are the kinds of scars I carry. Not as deep or traumatic as others—I am not unaware of the suffering of the world. But they are scars, nonetheless.

You know, I say, *you've given me lots of reasons to love you, and lots of reasons not to love you.*

She gives me a look. I love Ari's looks. She can say everything with a look. Her facial expressions are dissertations, novels, epic poems. In marriage counseling I talk, and she just looks. She is better understood than I.

I continue. *You can't really say you love someone until they give you a reason not to.*

Well, she says, I think I really love you.

Me too, I laugh. *I love it all. Scars and all.*

Scars?

Yeah, scars. I love those, too. Why do you love me?

It had taken me so long to learn this obvious thing about scars. They are not meant to be fixed or healed. They are scars. By definition, they won't go away. Our work is to bear witness to them, see them, love them.

God her scars are beautiful.

She gives me reasons why she loves me: I am kind, a good father, a good husband. I am smart. It's my resume, basically. *I can google myself, baby*, I laugh. (she gives me a look again, and I love it). *But what do you love now that you know it's all bullshit?*

I feel acutely now, as I haven't in years, the longing. I am scared, you see, afraid that I'm losing something that I hadn't even really contemplated it was possible to lose. And out of fear, I waver between intense anxiety, sleepless nights— taking me back to the lonely, sleepless, star-filled night of my childhood—only ameliorated by alcohol, and the pretending on which Ari insists, the pretending she learned as a means of coping since her early teens.

But I also learn to pay attention. *Why do I love this person?* It's a question seldom asked, because there seems to be no way to keep track of such things. And when we try, we go to the big things, the things that might show up on CV, or a Facebook page. "I love her because she's smart, beautiful, a good mother, etc."

But these are lies. Pay attention. You have to pay attention to really understand why you love someone. Because we never love anyone because they are a genius at the stock market; or because they write great books; or even because they are beautiful, or smart, or kind. *Pay attention.* It's the little things, the things that make no sense. The big things can be replaced. I can find another person who's smart like you, funny like you, beautiful like you. But there's no one else with the texture of your voice, your smell, your particularly charming brand of crazy.

Many years ago, I awoke with you next to me. It surprised me. I was used to being alone. Then, again, the next day, it happened again. Thousands of days later, it was still happening. It was that feeling of your body, its smell and its temperature, that keeps me hoping, each day, when I awake, that you are still there. These are all the little things, which, of course, are the only things: I love the touch of you, the smell of you, in the morning. Love the soft twang of Mississippi in your voice, the harsh edge of the south side in your tone. I even like when you make fun of me, as long as it makes you laugh.

I love the things you let me do for you. Like making bacon every morning, bacon that I, a vegetarian, will never eat. But I love to do this, love the smell of it, love to know that you will come down and eat what I've made with my hands, my heart.

I love making babies with you, raising babies with you. Love all those moments when we struggle together to figure out how to navigate raising three Black girls in a country that despises them.

I love the way you move when you dance, love your smile that lights up a room, a world. Mine anyway.

I love our memories: eating lunch outside of Assisi on our honeymoon and getting a ride home from strangers when it starts to rain; smoking on the fire escape in New York; our road trips, to Mexico, our move from California to Chicago.

I love those days when we ran retreats for the teens from Chicago, sitting by the fire telling them stories, love how hard you loved them, fought for them, knew them and their stories because you shared them.

There is a deeper kind of knowing a person that comes from the longing that emerges when the possibility of their absence becomes a reality. But when I feared that my marriage was ending, I began to pay attention. I came to experience the ultimate form of belonging, which emerges only when we can love another's scars. I had thought, for so long, that I could fix them, heal them. But the real answer was found in seeing that always, from the beginning, we had found one another, fit together, through a brokenness that we already shared. My task was to stop saving the world, to stop fixing her, and to heal my own brokenness, which, after all, was no different from the brokenness of the world, this little island floating through the cosmos, alone.

Our task, in the end, isn't to save the world, or the people close to us, but to figure out how to love it all, our people and our world, even when it's falling apart.

Our last week in Miami, Amira's youngest daughter, my goddaughter, arrives. She is only twenty-one, but about to be a college graduate, preparing to enter a PhD program to study philosophy. She is smart and thoughtful and full of questions and life. Her courage outweighs her fear. She is, Amira likes to say, all that Amira would have been had she been permitted a genuine childhood, if people had listened to her and let her fly. Ari often says similar things about Cosima.

I see her sitting on a bench. It's uncanny how her posture reminds me of her mother, her laugh of her auntie. Time is sometimes more circle than line, I think. Either way, it moves both too slow and too fast, and is bound, like us, only by love.

And also during our last week in Miami, the news comes from Chicago that Adam Toledo, a thirteen-year-old boy, was killed by the police. Although his hands were raised and empty when he was shot, the police and mayor focus on the fact that he had, at some point, had a gun. The blame is placed squarely on whoever it was who had put that gun in his hand. This makes me think. Cosima, like Adam, is a thirteen-year-old CPS student. What have we put in her hand? A book? A pen? A question? Have we put the tools in her hands for her to transform her world or herself? Have we given her things even heavier than a gun, but no less threatening, like entitlement, or fearlessness, or freedom, things that little whiteboys hold—like guns—without fearing being shot down by the police? But Adam wasn't merely given a gun. *He was given a story.* And whatever our children hold in their hands, its power lies in the story it tells—about who they are, their place in the world, about agency and power and joy. We give them a story that tells them how to love and be loved. And that is the story that determines their survival.

I think these things as I contemplate our return to Chicago, to our normal lives. The pandemic is slowing and we will get vaccines. What does normal even mean? What do we even want to return to? Is home a place? A person? Something in-between, ineffable?

On our way home, we pass through Asheville, where we got married. Memories come back like a flood. I am struck by how different it all is than what I imagined, how hard, but, still, how good. I walk through downtown with Cosima, showing her the hotel where Ari and I spent our wedding night. She is less annoyed than I expect. The air is cooler here, in this land defined by its old mountains rather than new restaurants and flat beaches. These mountains were one of the many things that Ari taught me to love. Through the mountains, I learned that we must get through the high places as well as the low, the cold mountain nights as well as the warm days at the beach, and that there is beauty in the hard and rough places—and even in the old. A marriage, like a mountain, teaches us that old love, well-worn and -earned, is its most beautiful form.

We have cut each other open in a thousand pieces with those broken parts that once fit together so perfectly. And now, as we consider this brokenness, I am scared of the unknown geometry of a new puzzle that is formed in healing. But I am still even more terrified of the prospect of your absence, a you-shaped hole in the universe that is bigger than the universe itself.

And that is a puzzle I cannot solve.

EPILOGUE: IN THIRTY YEARS
2051

Do you remember our winter in Miami? she will ask.

I will laugh. *How could I forget?*

We were crazy then, weren't we?

We had a lot to learn, didn't we?

I will talk, touching her gently under the covers. She'll complain about the position of the covers, the temperature. With her facial expressions, she'll say more than I can ever say. I don't really mind the complaints as long as her warm body is still in the bed every morning. Still there, after all these years.

Getting old will be hard, like childhood, adolescence, adulthood, middle age. A different kind of hard, but hard. But something in me knows it will be the best part, the part where I get to show her how beautiful she still is, even old and wrinkled. We'll still have a lot to learn, of course, but we'll know more than we know now.

The stories of Miami will be told and retold with all the other stories, remembered and forgotten again and again. Even as bodies fail and memories fade, we will have each other, and the possibility of listening and seeing, and maybe of even belonging. We will share this thing that's better than anything, even if we couldn't always give each other what was needed: We made a family, and a home, together.

Even when we've forgotten nearly everything, we will have the opportunity to re-encounter each other every day. There will always be something new, something we never quite knew. This is the gift of the struggle that comes from every encounter, if we pay attention. We never quite know another fully, and have the opportunity, every day, to learn something new.

What greater gift is there than this?

Tell me a story, I will say.

You know all my stories; you've heard them all.

What does that matter? What do you think I'm here for?

What *are* you here for? She'll tease me. I still don't know.

I'm here to hear your stories, the same old stories, over and over again.

ACKNOWLEDGMENTS

Writing a book such as this, which covers the breadth of a lifetime, it is impossible to put a limit on whom to thank. The interconnections are limitless, as is my gratitude. Nonetheless, some special mentions are in order:

Tim Brandhorst, Patrick Flynn, and Cosmos Boekell for your feedback. My parents, for many things, but especially for giving me the gift of literature. My brother. Sue and the Sue kids. Tony and the bagua brotherhood. Maxwell and the people who shared their food with me and drove me to Zimbabwe from Mozambique; the man who gave me an orange and a smile in Iran; and to all the people who gave me companionship and shelter on the road. Matthew Fox and the youth of YELLAWE and The Chicago Wisdom Project. The PCC department at CIIS. Connor Wolfe and Wayfarer Press for believing in me and this project. And always, my wife, my *Beatrice*, Arianne.

ABOUT THE AUTHOR

Theodore Richards (he/him) is a writer, philosopher, educator and founder of the Chicago Wisdom Project. He has received numerous literary awards, including three Independent Publisher Awards and two Nautilus Book Awards. *What Happened to Icarus* is his ninth book. He lives on the south side of Chicago with his wife and three daughters.

You can find out more about him and his work at www.theodorerichards.com.

Wayfarer Books is a fiercely independent, queer & trans-owned press publishing bold literature from the wild and societal margins.

At Wayfarer Books we believe poetry is the language of the earth. We believe words, like rivers through wild places, can change the shape of the world. We publish poets and writers and renegades who stand outside of mainstream culture; poets, essayists, and storytellers whose work might withstand the scrutiny of crows and coyotes, those who are cryptic and floral, the crepuscular, and the queer-at-heart. We are more than just a publisher but a community of writers. Our mission is to produce books that can serve as a compass and map to all wayfarers through wild terrain.

WAYFARERBOOKS.ORG

SUPPORTING INDIGENOUS FUTURES
1% GIVEN BACK

Wayfarer Books is based in the San Juan Mountains near Mesa Verde, on the lands of the Ancestral Pueblo, the Southern Ute, the Weenuchiu (the Mountain Ute), the Diné (Navajo), and the San Juan Southern Paiute Nations. We honor the generations of Indigenous communities who have stewarded these lands for thousands of years, and we acknowledge that this place was taken through colonization and displacement, and that Indigenous peoples remain present here, past and present. As one concrete act of accountability, we are launching 1% Given Back. Beginning now, we will give 1% of Wayfarer's net profits directly to the Indigenous nations whose lands we are based on, in support of sovereignty, Indigenous futures, and wealth redistribution. We do this in the belief that acknowledgment should move beyond words and into tangible practice.

www.ingramcontent.com/pod-product-compliance
Lightning Source LLC
LaVergne TN
LVHW041747060526
838201LV00046B/939